GOLFING IN THE CAROLINAS

ALSO BY WILLIAM PRICE FOX

Doctor Golf
Southern Fried
Moonshine Light, Moonshine Bright
Ruby Red
Southern Fried Plus Six
Dixiana Moon
Chitlin' Strut and Other Madrigals

GOLFING
in the Carolinas

BY WILLIAM PRICE FOX

JOHN F. BLAIR, PUBLISHER
WINSTON-SALEM, NORTH CAROLINA

MANUFACTURED BY WALSWORTH PRESS, INC., MARCELINE, MISSOURI

TYPESETTING BY THE COMPOSING ROOM OF MICHIGAN, GRAND RAPIDS, MICHIGAN
AND TYPOGRAPHY STUDIO, WINSTON-SALEM, NORTH CAROLINA

DESIGNED BY DEBRA L. HAMPTON

THIS BOOK IS PRINTED ON ACID-FREE PAPER

LIBRARY OF CONGRESS CATALOGING-IN-PUBLICATION DATA

Fox, William Price.
Golfing in the Carolinas / by William Price Fox.
p.   cm.
ISBN 0-89587-078-9
1. Golf courses— North Carolina. 2. Golf courses —South Carolina.
3. North Carolina— Description and travel— 1981- —Guide-books.
4. South Carolina— Description and travel— 1981- —Guide-books.
I. Title.
GV975.F65 1990
796.352'06'8756 —dc20   90-36695

For Kathy and Colin

CONTENTS

South Carolina

North Carolina

Acknowledgments

I'd like to thank the following for their help in putting this book together: Chip Russell at the Caravel; the Litchfield Inn; the Cal Harrelson Agency; the Newman, Saylor, and Gregory Agency; Dan Gleason of *Golf Georgia*; the Paul Himmelsback Agency; Cecil Brandon and Brandon Advertising and Sales, Inc.; Ansley D. Cohen III of Palmetto Dunes Resort; Arnold Langer of Marsan's International; and especially Parker Smith, the former senior editor of *Golf* magazine.

Preface

In 1989 at the Masters, there were over twelve hundred golf writers pounding out their burning stories on Nick Faldo of England and Seve Ballesteros, the Spaniard. Twelve hundred! Twelve hundred golf writers! Question. Can you name five golf writers? Three golf writers? One? Who, then, is this nameless, faceless society the IRS computer red-flags as questionable? Where do they come from? What do they do for a living?

First of all, we publish in *Golf, Golf Digest, Golf World, Golf Guide, Senior Golf, Junior Golf, Golf under the Lights,* and *Only Golf.* Failing these, the dailies, and failing those, the badly printed tour guides that crowd the "Take One, It's Free" racks at welcome centers.

With the exception of religious poetry, golf writing is probably the lowest-paid writing on the scene today. On the other hand, money isn't everything. There are other things, namely, free rooms, free meals, and free green fees. And public-relations and sales staffs, knowing the power of the written word, no matter what the publication, give us the best tee times and an occasional six-pack of name-brand balls. But of all the spinoffs, tradeoffs, and outright payoffs, the sweetest music to the ears of freeloading golf writers will always be books much like the one you have just opened. For having played all the courses and been to all the tournaments, if there's one thing we know, it's where the best courses are.

A couple of years back, I played in a foursome at Torquebrada, Spain, *behind* Sean Connery. The year before that, I played in Rabat, Morocco, in a foursome *behind* King Hassan II. I was a member of the Hollywood Hackers for three years and played *behind* Clint Eastwood, Jose Ferrer, Bill Bixby, and Jack Lemmon. But I've actually played *with* Larry Fine, one of the Three Stooges. I've also played in Hawaii, Paris, Biarritz, and Barcelona, and next year I'm doing a story on the driving ranges of Tokyo and another on a new nine-holer outside Moscow. So again, while there's very little money in golf writing, we get to rub elbows with the jet set, eat and drink for free, and play a lot of golf. And every March, we get to write it all off at tax time. Yes, it's lonely work, but someone has to do it.

The assignment for *Golfing in the Carolinas* was simply to pick out the fifty courses in the Carolinas that I liked best, play each of them, write a few words, and then go on to the next one. It turned out to be far more work and far more driving than I'm used to, and I discovered that North Carolina, from its northwest corner up near Linville to Wilmington on the coast, is as wide as Texas. I played so much golf that "overgolfing" set in, and my handicap soared from a twelve—which should be a nine—to a fifteen. I also wore out a set of grips and a pair of shoes, and I managed to lose a perfectly good Pinseeker sand wedge.

The odd thing was that the fifty courses I came up with by actually going and playing them—and in many cases waiting until the rain let up so I could play—are about the same fifty that most golf magazines come up with. But I learned many things on my tour, all about Donald Ross and Robert Trent Jones and Tom Fazio and Pete Dye, whom I watched working on a new course on Kiawah Island that will host the 1991 Ryder Cup match.

When all is said and done, Pete Dye's new course may turn out to be the most interesting in the Carolinas. It is being built on a peninsula and looks not unlike Portmarnock outside Dublin, the recent site of P. G. Carroll's Irish Open. And let's drop one more name here—I played a pro-am with Ireland's Christy O'Connor. O'Connor was the one who hit the 210-yard 2-iron stiff on the last hole to tie the Ryder Cup in 1989. Anyhow, Pete Dye's new course at Kiawah Island will have ten holes running right along the ocean, and it will have the same kind of wind that made Portmarnock famous. There's an old Scottish saying, "No wind, no golf." Well, there will be wind on Kiawah Island, and it will be blowing over what looks like it's going to be a one-of-a-kind masterpiece. Unfortunately, the course won't be seeded until this book is on the press.

I also learned that while North and South Carolina don't

have such venerables as Shinnecock and the Country Club at Brookline or Baltusrol, we have something else. We have Harbour Town and Linville Ridge and Pinehurst Number 2 and Long Cove and Haig Point. We also have a stunning Donald Ross course at Camden and my favorite, the Palmetto Club, the Alister Mackenzie layout in Aiken. When you consider that northern courses are closed four or five months a year and that down here in the so-called hard lard belt we play almost every day, you have to consider our advantages. And if you consider the enormous range of courses we have, from Linville Ridge, three thousand feet in elevation and carved right out of the mountains, to Pinehurst in the Sandhills, to Dataw Island and Seabrook Island on the ocean, the rest of the country simply pales by comparison.

I tried to judge the courses from the middle tees, the member tees. Where the pros tee up is another story, and one I think a lot of us should forget. Golf is about shot making, not course records or what this or that pro said about a course. A golfer will hit a dozen good shots in a round, and that's what he or she remembers. That's why golfers keep coming back and coming back; otherwise, the game will drive you crazy.

I have included a few courses connected to great hotels like the Grove Park Inn and the Greystone Inn in North Carolina and the Hyatt Hotel and the Mariners Inn at Palmetto Dunes on Hilton Head. On the other hand, many of the better private clubs that should have appeared here had no available photography or simply didn't want to be included, which is fair enough.

Anyhow, I've spent a long time on this project and loved almost every minute of it. The main thing I discovered was that from the mountains to the Sandhills to the Low Country, golf courses right here in North and South Carolina are, without any doubt or any qualification, the finest and the most available in the country.

The question always comes up as to which courses are the best of the best. I guess if I had to choose, I'd go with Pinehurst Number 2 and Wade Hampton in North Carolina and Harbour Town and Haig Point in South Carolina. If I had to choose two, I'd go with Pinehurst Number 2 and Harbour Town. And if one, Harbour Town. But when it gets right down to it, I guess you choose the course you played the best. In my case, that will always be Trenholm Road, a public nine-holer in Columbia that is no longer with us. It's a shopping mall. Three holes ran so closely alongside the road that cars would stop and wait for you to hit. And there wasn't a drop of water on the course—not even to drink. Anyhow, I broke the course record there. Not low gross or low net, but something else. I broke the number-of-holes-played record.

My buddy and I played twelve rounds one day—108 holes. We began at dawn, and when we were finishing, using flashlights so we could see to putt, we kept talking about how the club members would be there to help us celebrate, and how maybe a sports reporter from the *Columbia Record* would be there to make us famous. But when we came in, the only person there was the owner, who was sitting under a light reading a paperback novel and waiting to close up. I can still hear him now, hollering across the pitch-dark parking lot, "Y'all ain't going out again, are you?"

South Carolina

HAIG POINT

Haig Point

DAUFUSKIE ISLAND

Hilton Head Island

ATLANTIC OCEAN

P.O. Box 7319
Hilton Head Island, South Carolina 29938
803-686-2000

Private

Rees Jones, designer

Course Ratings

Calibogue Course M-74.6 L-73.1
Haig Point Course M-73.3 L-71.8

COURTESY OF HAIG POINT

A few years back, I said yes to a publicity stunt when I probably should have said no. All of a sudden in the middle of the night, I found myself on board the Strachan Mansion at St. Simons Island, Georgia. Built in 1910, the 7,500-square-foot home had been rescued from destruction by the International Paper Company, and it was to be barged a hundred miles up the Intracoastal Waterway to Daufuskie Island, south of Hilton Head. International Paper wanted the mansion for their centerpiece at the Haig Point golf resort. The move up the waterway was designed to attract great publicity.

The good news for International Paper was that the mansion cost them only one dollar. The bad news was that it ultimately cost them almost a million to move it. I was on board for the move, along with a couple of other writers. The publicity worked. Network television sent in helicopters to take footage of us squeezing under low bridges and waiting in the mud flats for the tide to change. You may have seen us sitting there in our deck chairs with our mint juleps, grinning and waving.

But when the cameras pulled back, we stopped smiling. We were getting desperate, for as we whipped up the waterway at speeds as great as two, three, and four knots, every mosquito in the Low Country had a shot at us. And they took it. All we could do was eat and drink and swat. We also prayed that the tides would be favorable and the trip would thereby be shortened.

Finally, after three long days and three long nights in a swamp where they should have shot *The African Queen*, we landed at Daufuskie. Stepping off the mansion, our eyes were red and our hands were trembling. We hadn't bothered to shave or even wash. We had lost the will to live. One of the International Paper executives, Ed Chazal by name, saw what had happened to us. A few months later, he invited us down for a weekend at the restored mansion.

I spent my time at the Haig Point resort in one

Calibogue Course

HOLE NUMBER	1	2	3	4	5	6	7	8	9	OUT	10	11	12	13	14	15	16	17	18	IN	TOT	HCP	NET
GOLD	380	419	415	582	190	445	398	192	528	3549	446	431	414	448	563	204	383	179	497	3565	7114		
WHITE	368	405	396	520	165	418	371	173	513	3329	438	415	391	409	549	196	366	171	482	3417	6746		
RED	340	374	365	490	152	397	338	161	499	3116	405	386	360	365	523	114	341	166	474	3134	6250		
HANDICAP	17	9	3	11	15	1	13	7	5		2	8	18	6	4	14	16	12	10				
PAR	4	4	4	5	3	4/5	4	3	5/4	36	4	4	4	4	5	3	4	3	5	36	72		
GREEN	317	346	343	435	145	371	290	127	486	2860	378	362	318	320	492	100	305	161	466	2902	5762		
HANDICAP	6	8	12	10	14	4	16	18	2		5	9	7	13	1	15	11	17	3				

COURTESY OF HAIG POINT

of the most tasteful and elegant rooms I have ever seen. I had five or six great meals in the mansion, and I played thirty-six holes of golf on what *Golf Digest* has ranked the twenty-eighth best course in the country and *Golf* magazine the sixty-eighth best in the world. So all in all, while I will never jump so quickly again when I'm offered a publicity tour, I guess International Paper knew what they were doing.

An old friend of mine from *Sports Illustrated*, Barry McDermott, came down a few years back and played the Rees Jones course. He was so impressed that he decided to move to the island. Since then, he has started working for the resort and now makes his living between golf assignments selling real estate. So if you plan to buy a place in the area, you might as well buy from someone who can help you with your game. Barry is a six. Tell him I sent you.

Mack Bridges, the pro at Haig Point, is world-famous back at Arcadian Shores for keeping a twelve-gauge shotgun under the counter. Guess what for? Wrong. He used it to shoot clubs thrown by players out of the trees—mostly putters.

MELROSE

MELROSE GOLF CLUB

P.O. Box 50
Daufuskie Island, South Carolina 29915
803-785-8584

Private

Jack Nicklaus, architect

Course Ratings

Gold 74.2
Blue 72.4
White 70.3
Red 72.1

PHOTOGRAPH BY PETE WINKEL COURTESY OF THE MELROSE COMPANY

Jack Nicklaus may be from Columbus, Ohio, but he seems to have found a home down on the barrier islands. In addition to his courses at Pawleys Plantation, Long Bay, and Turtle Point, he now has the Melrose Golf Course out on Daufuskie Island. Only a mile from Haig Point, Melrose is rapidly becoming one of the premier private country clubs in the entire country.

Daufuskie is the island where Pat Conroy held the teaching job that inspired his book *The Water is Wide*. It is also the place where humorist Lewis Grizzard tees up wearing his Georgia Bulldogs cap, shirt, jacket, and socks. I've never played with him, but the word is he has a unique hitch at the top of his swing. And some wag who knows him said that if there's ever a contest held for the member with the swing recognizable from the greatest distance, Lewis will be the man to beat. Also in attendance are Nicklaus, Ray Floyd, and tennis great Stan Smith. So much for the literati.

I've played Melrose once and it's not an easy course. Jack Nicklaus does not lay out an easy course. He seems to think that while everyone can't hit as long as he can, they should at least try. At Melrose, you are given that opportunity. From the gold back tees, the course stretches out to 7,052 hard yards. I'd advise not playing the gold tees unless the wind is completely down and the ground is hard enough to give you every inch of roll you deserve. You will also need a couple of shots bouncing down the cart paths to make the cut.

When the wind is up and it's soft, it's a different story altogether—a sadder story. Your only game then is from the middle tees. From there, it's a difficult 6,663 yards. You have to place your shots where Jack wants you to place them, and you have to putt like a demon. The greens are huge and undulating, and the fact that you're on in regulation means nothing.

Holes 17 and 18 are along the Atlantic Ocean, with the 18th predicted by Nicklaus to be one of the most photographed finishing holes ever designed. When I played it and pushed a shot onto the beach and had to recover from the drift-

HOLE NUMBER	1	2	3	4	5	6	7	8	9	OUT	10	11	12	13	14	15	16	17	18	IN	TOT	NET
GOLD TEES	395	435	544	411	215	430	398	136	584	3548	400	383	525	184	460	405	187	400	560	3504	7052	
BLUE TEES	380	412	522	395	186	412	373	127	561	3368	371	355	513	168	431	390	170	371	526	3295	6663	
WHITE TEES	363	389	488	372	162	385	352	112	498	3112	350	339	480	151	412	374	148	350	495	3099	6211	
PAR	4	4	5	4	3	4	4	3	5	36	4	4	5	3	4	4	3	4	5	36	72	
HANDICAP	15	3	9	13	5	11	7	17	1		14	18	10	8	4	6	16	12	2			
RED TEES	334	366	471	336	140	321	322	73	463	2826	333	318	443	128	381	347	128	333	452	2863	5689	

18TH HOLE

PHOTOGRAPH BY PETE WINKEL
COURTESY OF THE MELROSE COMPANY

wood, I felt like I was in the original pterodactyl burying ground.

The focal point of Melrose is a stunning fifty-two-room structure patterned after the original Melrose Plantation. Forty-six of the rooms offer an ocean view, and verandas on the main floor look out over the front lawn and the rose gardens.

There is no bridge from Hilton Head to Daufuskie Island, but Melrose members have their own ferryboat fleet, which features a hundred-passenger ferry and two fifty-passenger boats. But the best news besides the great Nicklaus course and the beautiful mansion is the simple fact that there will never be a bridge out here. For isolation, a beach club, a golf course, a Stan Smith Tennis Center, and probably the perfect way to live, ladies and gentlemen, boys and girls, if this isn't it, it isn't out there.

Country Club
of Hilton Head

70 Skull Creek Drive
Hilton Head Island, South Carolina 29926
803-681-4653

Semi-Private

Rees Jones, architect

Course Ratings

Gold 73.6
Blue 71.7
White 70.0

8TH HOLE

PHOTOGRAPH BY PETE WINKEL COURTESY OF THE MELROSE COMPANY

1 2

Rees Jones created one of his greatest layouts for the Country Club of Hilton Head. While the course is demanding from the member tees, it turns into an avenging monster from the blues. On each hole, Jones gives you a different test and a different view of the oak groves, the pine forests, and the salt marsh through which this beautiful course meanders. Some holes close in tightly around you, but then suddenly you're looking out over a panorama of salt marsh, blue water, and sailboats on Skull Creek.

The other facilities on the premises include a first-class driving range, a putting green, a chipping green, and a practice bunker. There is also a nine-hole, executive-length Cayman course where you can warm up. Or if you're getting the message that you're not ready to take on the big course, you can play another round on the Cayman. And then another round. All the facilities are in view of the expansive clubhouse, which is equipped with everything from tennis courts to indoor and outdoor pools.

I played the big course recently with three doctors who had come down from Cleveland for a convention. It's good to know that, as a group, the medical profession doesn't produce too many touring pros. I mean, if I knew a brain surgeon who had a one handicap, he'd be the last person on earth I'd be seeing about a headache.

Anyhow, the pediatrician would hook, and the nose-and-throat specialist would slice. The radiologist, who stood five-foot-two and must have weighed 240, had to open his stance ninety degrees to get his hands and arms through the shot. When he was able to hitch his stomach out of the way, he hit it down the middle about 140 yards. When he couldn't, he whiffed. It was a long, long day, and at one point I looked over and the nose-and-throat guy had gone to sleep in the cart. When we finally dragged in—we had to call it off because of darkness—we went straight to the bar. And we stayed there.

Now the great thing about golf was what fol-

HOLE NUMBER	1	2	3	4	5	6	7	8	9	OUT	10	11	12	13	14	15	16	17	18	IN	TOT	HCP	NET
GOLD	398	413	166	431	358	491	171	518	433	3379	423	184	575	438	185	378	376	402	579	3540	6919		
BLUE	365	393	156	407	338	467	143	496	410	3175	396	178	540	415	160	358	373	392	556	3368	6543		
WHITE	335	364	130	384	326	461	133	487	398	3018	388	151	511	401	152	351	358	286	546	3144	6162		
HANDICAP	11	7	17	3	13	9	15	5	1		2	16	6	4	18	10	12	14	8				
PAR	4	4	3	4	4	5	3	5	4	36	4	3	5	4	3	4	4	4	5	36	72		
RED	310	336	94	364	301	405	103	460	372	2745	360	115	480	393	70	328	342	273	507	2868	5613		
HANDICAP	13	11	17	9	5	3	15	1	7		8	16	4	6	18	12	10	14	2				

17TH HOLE

PHOTOGRAPH BY PETE WINKEL
COURTESY OF THE MELROSE COMPANY

lowed. For the next three hours, all we did was imitate each other's swings and make fun of our games. In short, we had much more fun after the round than during it. And the nice thing was that almost every person in the bar joined in. Maybe that's why this crazy game keeps bringing us back. So whether you're a high handicapper or a low handicapper, or even a member of the medical profession, you'll feel more than welcome at the Country Club of Hilton Head, especially in the bar.

Long Cove Club

SOUTH
CAROLINA

278

HILTON
HEAD
ISLAND

Long Cove
Club

ATLANTIC OCEAN

44 Long Cove Drive
Hilton Head Island, South Carolina 29928
803-842-5558

Private

Pete Dye, designer

Course Ratings

Gold 74.3
Blue 71.9
White 69.9
White (L) 74.6
Red 69.5

PHOTOGRAPH BY E. CORNELL COURTESY OF LONG COVE CLUB

1 6

Ancient historians listed seventeen reasons why the Roman Empire fell to the invading Goths and Visigoths, but they missed the real reason, which every Southern golfer has always known. The Goths and Visigoths simply wanted a little more sunshine and about eighty to a hundred feet of beachfront property. Such is the history of almost every northern country whose citizens tire of snow and cloud cover and golf courses that are frozen from November to March. And that is precisely why Hilton Head has done nothing but grow since Charles Fraser landed here and planted the flag.

For the past fifteen years, South Carolina has always placed two or three golf courses in the top hundred in the country. Today, owing to three new courses on Hilton Head, the number is six, with two or three others closing in fast. Long Cove Club, a Pete Dye layout built in 1983, is one of the newcomers. It has already moved into the top twenty. With its stunning views of the Intracoastal Waterway and its natural set-ting, the course has a distinctly Scottish quality. The fairways are boldly contoured, and the undulating greens are surrounded by everything up to and including grass mounds, pot bunkers, and sand bunkers. And the greens are more than just big—they are enormous. The 18th measures 210 feet across, which throws a brand-new wrinkle at most golfers—namely, the 100- to 150-foot putt. I had one recently on the 18th, and I recall taking a big backswing and almost a full pivot.

On the business side at Long Cove, the manager and broker in charge is John E. "Bubba" McKenzie, an old friend of mine who began his working life as a lifeguard on Hilton Head when it first opened up. He likes to tell the story of how, when he first started showing property on the island, fifteen wild hogs surrounded his Jeep and he had to climb onto the roof until help came. With a man named Bubba, you've got to divide by three, but even five red-eyed, wild, gnashing hogs are a lot of hogs. Anyhow, Long

HOLE NUMBER	1	2	3	4	5	6	7	8	9	OUT	10	11	12	13	14	15	16	17	18	IN	TOT	HCP	NET
GOLD TEES	400	196	539	384	317	513	439	203	428	3419	403	376	445	137	410	590	460/429	210/186	450/441	3481/3417	6900/6836		
BLUE TEES	390	151	527	359	290	509	430	195	375	3226	387	368	397	130	374	557	389	172	420	3194	6420		
WHITE TEES	358	145	503	344	276	498	388	155	329	2996	346	326	379	116	352	495	354	143	366	2877	5873		
HANDICAP	7	17	1	11	13	5	3	15	9		10	14	4	18	6	2	12	16	8				
PAR	4	3	5	4	4	5	4	3	4	36	4	4	4	3	4	5	4	3	4	35	71		
RED TEES	334	94	446	294	239	425	308	117	272	2529	296	311	313	84	291	439	311	116	312	2473	5002		
HANDICAP	5	17	1	9	13	3	7	15	11		14	10	4	18	6	2	12	16	8				

Cove is not only one of the great courses on Hilton Head, it's one of the great courses in the country. If you're down this way, make a few phone calls and get on it. It's a course you'll never forget.

THE ROBERT TRENT JONES GOLF CLUB AT

PALMETTO DUNES®

SOUTH
CAROLINA

278

HILTON
HEAD
ISLAND

**Robert Trent Jones
Golf Club at
Palmetto Dunes**

ATLANTIC OCEAN

P.O. Box 5849
Hilton Head Island, South Carolina 29928
803-785-1138

Semi-Private

Robert Trent Jones, designer

Course Ratings

Blue   72.2
White   69.3
Red   70.7

PHOTOGRAPH BY BRIAN MORGAN   COURTESY OF GREENWOOD DEVELOPMENT CORPORATION

Hilton Head has many things to offer, but the main attractions are the greatest concentration of outstanding courses and the very best accommodations in the country. All told, there are twenty-three courses on the big island and neighboring Daufuskie Island, with four more on the drawing board. Three of them—namely, Melrose, Long Cove, and Haig Point—are for members and their guests only. All of which brings me to the three courses at Palmetto Dunes, which are available to guests of the hotels and villas.

Palmetto Dunes is a two-thousand-acre resort with three championship courses, the nationally acclaimed Rod Laver Tennis Center, a deepwater marina, and over three miles of uninterrupted beach. What a dedicated golfer would want to do with a marina, tennis courts, or a beach when the Robert Trent Jones Course, the George Fazio Course, and the Arthur Hills Course are all within a thousand yards is beyond me. But if you don't want to play, there they are, the beach and the marina.

The oldest course at Palmetto Dunes is the Robert Trent Jones. The twenty-year-old layout weaves in and out among creeks and lagoons and offers unexpected and stunning views of the broad, white beach, the ocean, and dolphins and shrimp boats cruising along the coast. I've played the Robert Trent Jones five or six times, and each time it's been a joy to see a course that stays in great shape.

While there is a Palmetto Dunes Club private membership, and the feeling is definitely of a private club, all three courses are open year-round to the public. Guests at the Hyatt Hotel and the Mariner's Inn are given preferential tee times and reduced rates. They may also walk after 2:00 P.M.

While the Hyatt Hotel and the Mariner's Inn are stunning places to stay, I prefer the more informal villas at Palmetto Dunes, which are ideal for families. The villas are centrally located, the three courses are at your doorstep, and the food, service, and general ambiance are excellent. The villas are like a giant, two-story hotel

HOLE NUMBER	1	2	3	4	5	6	7	8	9	OUT	10	11	12	13	14	15	16	17	18	IN	TOT	HCP	NET
BLUE	435	383	323	539	201	397	401	198	510	3387	540	376	154	380	417	506	378	179	390	3320	6707		
WHITE	404	364	311	507	159	371	378	159	483	3136	482	347	138	283	385	488	350	156	366	2995	6131		
HANDICAP	1	5	9	7	17	3	11	8	13		10	8	18	14	2	12	6	16	4				
PAR	4	4	4	5	3	4	4	3	5	36	5	4	3	4	4	5	4	3	4	36	72		
RED	342	350	319	461	113	340	361	92	444	2822	433	242	102	256	359	460	323	91	337	2603	5425		
HANDICAP	11	5	7	3	17	13	9	15	1		2	14	16	10	12	4	8	18	6				

spread out around twenty-five pools; the result is that every three or four villas have semiprivate swimming. You have the choice of renting a two- or three-bedroom villa facing the tennis courts, the golf courses, or the ocean. You can even rent one on a creek, with a free canoe tossed in. And if you have enough Boy Scout merit badges, you can pack your sticks carefully in the middle of your canoe and paddle to a course.

THE GEORGE FAZIO GOLF CLUB AT

PALMETTO DUNES®

SOUTH CAROLINA

278

HILTON HEAD ISLAND

George Fazio Golf Club at Palmetto Dunes

ATLANTIC OCEAN

P.O. Box 5849
Hilton Head Island, South Carolina 29928
803-785-1138

Semi-Private

George Fazio, designer

Course Ratings

Gold	74.2
Blue	72.6
White	71.2
Red	69.2

PHOTOGRAPH BY BRIAN MORGAN   COURTESY OF GREENWOOD DEVELOPMENT CORPORATION

2 4

The second course at Palmetto Dunes is the George Fazio Course, right across the road from the Robert Trent Jones. The Fazio has appeared on *Golf Digest*'s list of America's top hundred courses. It is not an easy layout. As a matter of fact, it has a 71.2 USGA rating at only 6,239 yards from the middle tees, while the Robert Trent Jones has a 69.3 at 6,131 yards. The reason is that the Fazio has tighter fairways combined with small, elevated greens, always a deadly combination. On ten holes, the lagoons and creeks come into play, and when there's no water to play over, yawning sand traps gobble up almost any stray shot.

With only two par-5s, the heart of the course is a series of long par-4s. And they are long: 393, 412, 422, 409, 414, 416, and 445 from the middle tees. And with the small greens looking even smaller when you're trying to hit them with a 2-iron or a 3-wood, the holes play much longer than they measure. If you're playing well, try the Fazio. If you're not, play the Robert Trent

Jones first and work out your problems. The Fazio is one course where you don't want to be doing any experimenting.

The Fazio also offers a severe challenge to the low handicapper playing the back tees, from which the layout measures 6,873 very hard yards.

I've played here three times from the middle tees, and I've yet to break 90. The last four holes, which come in at 414, 416, 210, and 445, have wiped me out every time. But it's a gorgeous course, and one day when the sky is clear and the bluebirds are singing and I'm not hooking off the tee, I'll be out there on it again.

And speaking of hooking, the pros at the Robert Trent Jones and the Fazio are probably the best in the country for lessons. Whether you're a seasoned player or a fledgling, there is a marvelous three-day golf school that covers all phases of the game, offering private playing instruction and individual video lessons. Or better yet if you're trying to save money, there is a big

HOLE NUMBER	1	2	3	4	5	6	7	8	9	OUT	10	11	12	13	14	15	16	17	18	IN	TOT	HCP	NET
GOLD	432	562	412	205	389	180	414	431	421	3446	513	394	387	386	185	445	425	230	462	3427	6873		
BLUE	393	522	412	195	372	167	374	422	409	3266	513	376	364	366	164	414	416	210	445	3268	6534		
WHITE	385	487	396	190	364	156	359	421	385	3143	485	364	319	354	150	410	403	187	424	3096	6239		
HANDICAP	3	11	9	15	7	17	5	1	13		18	10	14	8	16	6	4	12	2				
PAR	4	5	4	3	4	3	4	4	4	35	5	4	4	4	3	4	4	3	4	35	70		
RED	355	412	357	137	295	136	320	342	321	2675	438	320	275	279	123	342	349	122	350	2598	5273		
HANDICAP	5	1	11	15	13	17	9	3	7		2	10	12	14	18	6	8	16	4				

discount for groups of two or three. There is also a club-repair shop that can regrip your old clubs, reshaft them, change their swing weights, and shorten or lengthen them.

My best memory of the Fazio is not the string of 90s I posted or the birdie I had on the impossible 445-yard 18th. It was the fact that, after I'd lost my wedge out on the course, it showed up at my home in Columbia three days later. It had been lovingly packed in polyethylene pellets, and there was no charge.

THE ARTHUR HILLS GOLF CLUB AT

PALMETTO DUNES®

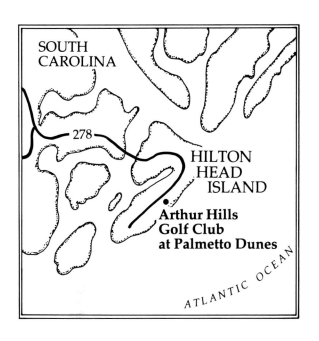

SOUTH
CAROLINA

278

HILTON
HEAD
ISLAND

**Arthur Hills
Golf Club
at Palmetto Dunes**

ATLANTIC OCEAN

P.O. Box 5849
Hilton Head Island, South Carolina 29928
803-785-1138

Semi-Private

Arthur Hills, designer

Course Ratings

Blue	71.4
White	69.3
Red	68.2

PHOTOGRAPH BY BRIAN MORGAN   COURTESY OF GREENWOOD DEVELOPMENT CORPORATION

Opened for play in the spring of 1986, the Arthur Hills Course is one of the most distinctive layouts in the Hilton Head area. It is blessed with a unique seaside character, with dune lines continuing from the fairways to the undulating surfaces of the greens, creating a brand-new look in golf course design. The dune lines have given the course a dramatic, rolling effect and big, interesting greens. Arthur Hills built the tee boxes up high and used the natural elevations beautifully.

Hills is very pleased with his layout at Palmetto Dunes, and he is especially fond of the windmill landmark on the 5th. The dunes allowed him to tone down the rough and use only a few sand traps. The difficulty of the course comes from off-balance lies and the lagoons that come into play. And speaking of lagoons, you are either playing alongside or over one on ten holes.

Recently, I had a chance to play a few holes with Arthur Hills at a golf outing. While he is from the Midwest, he seems to have caught on to the ways of the South and is rapidly becoming one of the most popular architects around. He has just finished the first nine of an eighteen-hole layout at Morgan Creek over on Dataw Island, and he is working on three or four other Southern layouts.

As for Hills's game, he plays a six handicap and has a smooth, drowsy backswing and a picture-perfect finish. On the day we played together, he was testing out a new hole on Dataw Island. He played it over and over again to determine whether the second shot, which has to go over a tree, made a fair demand on golfers, or whether he should take the tree out. After he played the hole seven or eight times—with about a 210-yard drive with no roll down the

HOLE NUMBER	1	2	3	4	5	6	7	8	9	OUT	10	11	12	13	14	15	16	17	18	IN	TOT	HCP	NET
BLUE COURSE	384	373	146	430	376	505	434	156	518	3322	415	182	399	507	412	153	365	380	516	3329	6651		
WHITE COURSE	358	334	115	403	343	480	417	135	494	3079	392	132	377	486	361	142	336	320	497	3042	6122		
MEN'S HDCP.	13	3	17	11	5	9	1	15	7		14	16	2	6	10	18	8	4	12				
PAR	4	4	3	4	4	5	4	3	5	36	4	3	4	5	4	3	4	4	5	36	72		
RED COURSE	284	289	88	294	301	410	322	113	434	2535	312	114	296	338	301	120	295	274	414	2464	4999		
LADIES' HDCP.	15	1	17	9	3	11	7	13	5		14	16	2	8	10	18	12	4	6				

PHOTOGRAPH BY BRIAN MORGAN
COURTESY OF GREENWOOD DEVELOPMENT CORPORATION

middle and a high 9-iron over the big live oak—he said he was satisfied that the shot was fair and that he would be able to keep the tree. To me, that is the way to lay out a course, and it was the same philosophy that prevailed at the Arthur Hills Course at Palmetto Dunes. What particularly endeared Mr. Hills to me, however, was the fact that after he was hole high in two on the par-4, he proceeded to three-putt for a bogie. And so it goes.

AT SEA PINES PLANTATION

SOUTH CAROLINA

278

HILTON HEAD ISLAND

Harbour Town Golf Links at Sea Pines Plantation

ATLANTIC OCEAN

P.O. Box 7000
Hilton Head Island, South Carolina 29938
803-671-2446

Semi-Private

Pete Dye, Course Architect
Jack Nicklaus, Design Consultant

Course Ratings

Heritage	74.0
Men	70.0
Ladies	69.0

PHOTOGRAPH BY HUGH OWEN, MEMORIES BY OWEN   COURTESY OF SEA PINES PLANTATION

About ten years back, I played in the Heritage Pro-Am and had an 82 and an 81. While my scores from the middle tees didn't exactly bring the course to its knees, they did represent a landmark in perseverance and a lesson in golf that should not go unreported.

The grim fact was that I arrived on Hilton Head on a cold, blowing day with a rampaging virus and a fever of 101. On the 1st tee, standing at the ball washer, I asked the Lord to just let me hit anywhere as long as I didn't throw up in front of the gallery. And the Lord (I knew it was the Lord because He sounded like John Houseman) told me to take my swing back on the outside, pause, and swing easily, and He'd see what He could do.

Well, I'm here to tell you that He came through and that I've never played better. It was during the tournament and the festivities afterwards and the parties in between that I fell in love with Harbour Town Golf Links at Sea Pines Plantation, the Heritage Pro-Am, and every-thing else on Hilton Head up to and including the Huddle House.

The most famous eighteen here is, of course, Harbour Town. The course is a Pete Dye master-piece noted for its small greens and narrow fair-ways. Phrases like "You have to walk down the fairways single file" were coined at Harbour Town. Not only are the fairways tight and the greens small, but the jungle they call the rough supposedly led one player to announce that he wouldn't go in there to save his own children. Many pros simply leave their drivers in their cars, because if the ball isn't straight, it's in trouble.

Alligators up to fifteen or sixteen feet in length thrive among the creeks and lakes at Sea Pines Plantation, as do raccoons and deer. In the eve-nings, possums (the small dogs that do not bark) pad from one house to the next looking for handouts. And if you stand still long enough at night, there's a chance of seeing an owl.

The lighthouse at the 18th green is the center-

HOLE NUMBER	1	2	3	4	5	6	7	8	9	OUT	10	11	12	13	14	15	16	17	18	IN	TOT	HCP	NET
HERITAGE	414	505	411	198	535	419	180	462	337	3461	436	438	413	378	165	575	376	192	478	3451	6912		
MEN	328	481	342	160	515	379	140	422	310	3077	352	392	383	335	138	507	316	161	458	3042	6119		
HANDICAP	13	9	15	11	3	5	17	1	7		10	4	8	12	18	6	16	14	2				
PAR	4	5	4	3	5	4	3	4	4	36	4	4	4	4	3	5	4	3	4	35	71		
LADIES	300	420	297	131	432	304	94	353	275	2606	326	314	290	302	97	417	240	97	330	2413	5019		
HANDICAP	7	3	11	17	1	13	15	5	9		6	10	14	4	16	2	12	18	8				

18TH HOLE

COURTESY OF SEA PINES PLANTATION

piece of the Harbour Town course. The par-4 16th, the tight, par-3 17th, and the ocean-bordered, par-4 18th leading up to the lighthouse have been staples on network television since the seventies.

Harbour Town—on everybody's list of the top twenty-five courses in the world and a recent host of the Nabisco Championship, with its $450,000 first prize and $2 million total purse—has been the home of the Heritage Golf Classic since the late seventies. With tickets harder and harder to come by at the Masters, played a week after the Heritage, a lot of us are simply coming down to see the Heritage and staying and playing the next week, then watching what happens in Augusta on the clubhouse television. Try it, but make your room reservations early.

THE OCEAN COURSE AT

SEA PINES®

PLANTATION

SOUTH
CAROLINA

278

HILTON
HEAD
ISLAND

**The Ocean Course at
Sea Pines Plantation**

ATLANTIC OCEAN

P.O. Box 7000
Hilton Head Island, South Carolina 29938
1-800-845-6131

Semi-Private

George Cobb, designer

Course Ratings

Blue   71
White   70
Red   70

15TH HOLE

PHOTOGRAPH BY FRED MOLLANE   COURTESY OF SEA PINES PLANTATION

To begin at the beginning, the Ocean Course at Sea Pines Plantation on Hilton Head is where it all began in the early sixties. Today, there are twenty-five courses within twenty-odd miles, with four more on the drawing board. But the Ocean Course was the flagship and the wake it created has been rolling ever since. Thanks to the Ocean Course, the world has come to know that there are islands off the coast of South Carolina, that those islands are, with the grace of air conditioning, habitable, and that you can play golf between 360 and 362 days a year.

With the possible exception of the 18th at Pebble Beach, the 15th here is probably the most-photographed hole in the world. Back in the sixties, when the sports magazines wanted to show a Hilton Head hole that overlooked the ocean, the only shot that John Gettys Smith, the course's public-relations director, had was one of the 15th. "The magazines were driving me crazy to get Charles Fraser to get another course started," Smith said. "They were tired of using the same shot over and over again. But that's all

we had and that's what they kept showing. But you know something, it's still a pretty hole."

I played the Ocean Course with a comic named Kirby who had never been north of Tahoe or east of Vegas. He had never been to a zoo, and the only alligators he had ever seen were in the movies. I told him I could guarantee that he would see at least a dozen alligators when we played here, so we loaded up the cooler and drove down from Columbia.

Perhaps the cloud cover was too thick or too thin or the pollen count was wrong, but for some reason we didn't see a thing except egrets, pelicans, doves, and pileated woodpeckers for sixteen holes. Finally, on the 17th, long after Kirby had decided that there was no such thing as an alligator, there beside a lagoon lay a monster that looked longer than my Ford Fairlane.

Kirby looked at it and began laughing. It was so big and so asleep he thought it was something plastic from Disney World that I'd had some redneck buddies blow up for his benefit. Before I could stop him, he was prodding the

HOLE NUMBER	1	2	3	4	5	6	7	8	9	OUT	10	11	12	13	14	15	16	17	18	IN	TOT	HCP	NET
CHAMPIONSHIP	327	439	173	484	330	408	216	395	495	3267	370	169	378	355	475	207	449	536	408	3347	6614		
MEN'S	311	382	149	471	309	394	201	372	478	3067	349	154	351	332	461	190	423	523	363	3146	6213		
HANDICAP	13	1	15	11	17	3	5	7	9		12	18	14	8	16	10	2	4	6				
PAR	4	4	3	5	4	4	3	4	5	36	4	3	4	4	5	3	4	5	4	36	72		
LADIES'	289	351	115	424	266	324	179	329	423	2700	256	136	282	305	416	127	323	426	313	2584	5284		
HANDICAP	9	1	17	3	13	7	11	15	5		14	18	12	2	8	16	6	4	10				

18TH HOLE

beast with his putter. And then two strange things happened simultaneously. The alligator's mouth opened, and the monster made a hissing, rushing lunge. Kirby did a quickstep and levitated two or three feet. He did some aerial acrobatics, hit the ground running, and didn't turn around until he was a hundred yards down the fairway. He was no longer laughing, and I was the one who had to go back and get the putter.

Yes, Virginia, there are alligators down here, along with great golf and a friendly group at the bar. Try it. You can't go wrong.

Wexford
W
PLANTATION

SOUTH CAROLINA

278

HILTON HEAD ISLAND

Wexford Plantation

ATLANTIC OCEAN

P.O. Box 6525
Hilton Head Island, South Carolina 29938
803-686-8812

Private

Willard Byrd, designer

Course Ratings

Blue 73.2
White 71.1
Green 68.4
Red 70.0

WEXFORD PLANTATION, HILTON HEAD ISLAND, SOUTH CAROLINA

PHOTOGRAPH BY BILL LITTELL

One of the big success stories on Hilton Head is the phenomenal growth of the Wexford Village community, which has as its centerpiece the beautiful, Willard Byrd–designed Wexford Plantation golf club. Wexford is an exclusive private club for property owners and their guests only, but its reputation has spread around the entire world. This is evidenced by the fact that property owners have come from all over, including such golfing outposts as Italy, Greece, West Germany, Portugal, and South America.

The outstanding environmental planning at Wexford is based on the formula that only 40 percent of the five hundred acres of land should be used for homesites. The rest has been left in marshlands. Lagoons and the Intracoastal Waterway wind their way through the moss-draped live oaks, the sweet gums, and the magnolias.

Recently, I had a chance to fly over Wexford in a helicopter. From a thousand feet, the course is stunning, and the par-4 9th looks like a hole that a golfer with a fade would be better off just picking up and walking. But down on the 9th tee, you quickly see that Willard Byrd had a soft spot in his heart for faders and slicers, as the fairway to the left is wide open for a safe shot. And the sand that lines the entire fairway often saves golfers from a worse, watery fate.

Wexford is laid out along the waterway. It may be the only course in the world where you can play the front nine, stop off at your boat anchored in the marina for some refreshments, and then play the back nine.

At the heart of the Wexford community is a 37.5-acre harbor, protected by a system of locks that provides a minimum depth of eight feet, as well as the comforts of security and privacy. The boatslips can accommodate yachts up to seventy-five feet in length. The layout of the community of private homes—which range in price from $450,000 to $2 million—allows residents to moor their yachts at the back door.

Not long ago, a convoy of boats left Wexford Harbor loaded down with golfers, their spouses,

HOLE NUMBER	1	2	3	4	5	6	7	8	9	OUT	10	11	12	13	14	15	16	17	18	IN	TOT	HCP	NET
BLUE	378	404	177	418	542	170	378	545	389	3401	412	558	442	162	381	554	410	187	380	3486	6887		
WHITE	359	383	158	389	514	153	364	507	366	3193	391	525	409	142	352	525	370	175	312	3201	6394		
GREEN	332	355	140	353	487	138	341	480	340	2966	336	491	353	122	334	488	330	141	281	2876	5842		
HANDICAP	13	9	17	3	1	15	11	5	7		8	6	4	18	16	2	10	14	12				
PAR	4	4	3	4	5	3	4	5	4	36	4	5	4	3	4	5	4	3	4	36	72		
RED	300	327	120	335	452	121	296	444	332	2727	288	445	287	94	294	444	308	120	225	2505	5232		
HANDICAP	13	11	15	7	1	17	9	3	5		10	4	12	18	14	2	8	16	6				

their sticks, and two or three bottles of sherry. The cruise took them to Bohicket Marina, where they anchored for the evening. The following morning, they had their choice of golf at either Seabrook or Kiawah islands. The nongolfers were driven into Charleston, twenty miles away, for a sightseeing tour. After another night at Bohicket, the convoy set sail for Calibogue Marina, where the participants stopped for another night, played golf at Harbour Town, had dinner at Sea Pines Plantation, and then cruised back home. And if there is a better way to live than that, it has yet to come to my attention.

9TH HOLE
WEXFORD GOLF CLUB

PHOTOGRAPH BY SKIP MEACHEN

CALLAWASSIE

THE COUNTRY CLUB OF CALLAWASSIE

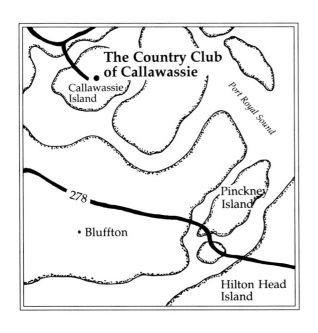

P.O. Box 22421
Hilton Head Island, South Carolina 29938
803-842-4955

Semi-Private

Tom Fazio, architect

Course Ratings

Gold 73.2
Blue 70.9
White 69.0
Red 70.1

PHOTOGRAPH BY J. LAFAYETTE COURTESY OF BRIGHT ADVERTISING

Fifteen minutes from Beaufort, or thirty from Hilton Head, or forty from Savannah, Georgia, lies the 880-acre island called Callawassie. The old Indian name means "beautiful island," and the Indians were right on the money. Indian shell rings that date back ten thousand years can be found on the island, along with oyster-shell "tabby" ruins from the plantation era.

The Country Club of Callawassie is rapidly developing into one of the most prestigious golf courses and golf communities in the entire country. Strict covenants guarantee that no public restaurants, hotels, motels, or stores will ever clutter the place, which in turn guarantees there will be no All You Can Eat neon signs flashing in the night.

Callawassie is blessed with a wonderful forest of palmetto trees, magnolias, and hundred-year-old live oaks, and with a rolling terrain that reaches some eighteen feet above sea level. That elevation allowed Tom Fazio to create a stunning layout complete with swales, dunes, deep-faced bunkers, and waste bunkers, giving the course a very distinctive Scottish look. At the same time, the old tabby ruins and the Spanish moss–draped oaks and magnolias let you know that, while it might look a little like Scotland, you are definitely in the land of Gullah, shrimp boats, and she-crab soup. As a matter of fact, not too far down the road is the town of Pocataligo (poke a turtle's tail and he will go), which is about as Gullah as you can get.

The 17th and 18th holes at Callawassie are considered by many to be the most breathtaking and heartbreaking finishing holes in golf. Believe me, I know it for a fact. I've played the course twice: once from the middle tees, at 6,035 yards, and once from the back, at 6,956. Playing from the back tees was a terrible mistake because the water, which barely comes into play from the middle tees, snagged a couple of perfectly good drives. In other words, I was often lying three when I should have been lying one. In other words, I had an 83 from the middle tees

HOLE NUMBER	1	2	3	4	5	6	7	8	9	OUT	10	11	12	13	14	15	16	17	18	IN	TOT	HCP	NET
GOLD	351	372	199	378	548	206	585	396	376	3411	384	556	229	441	358	182	400	606	389	3545	6956		
BLUE	337	350	191	361	515	185	555	361	332	3187	352	532	181	396	347	168	365	565	369	3275	6462		
WHITE	322	323	183	329	491	160	529	348	297	2982	346	520	157	371	331	149	334	542	303	3053	6035		
HANDICAP	18	6	12	10	4	8	2	14	16		17	3	11	5	13	15	9	1	7				
PAR	4	4	3	4	5	3	5	4	4	36	4	5	3	4	4	3	4	5	4	36	72		
RED	263	273	152	303	414	127	475	305	253	2565	308	447	137	322	266	137	279	485	255	2636	5201		
HANDICAP	18	6	12	10	4	8	2	14	16		17	3	11	5	13	15	9	1	7				

and a 94 from the back. The 94 could have been much higher, but I snaked in two thirty-footers for sixes instead of eights. After those putts dropped, I decided that Callawassie possesses the finest greens on the entire seaboard.

Tom Fazio, the gentleman who gave the world Wade Hampton up in Cashiers and the Wachesaw Club over at Murrells Inlet, has used the course elevation at Callawassie beautifully for the tee boxes and the raised greens. The remarkable layout is one to be played over and over again. *Golf Digest* has consistently rated it in the top five in South Carolina. I'll go along with that.

DATAW ISLAND

COTTON DIKE COURSE

One Club Road
Dataw Island, South Carolina 29920
803-838-3838

Private

Tom Fazio, designer

Course Ratings

Blue 73.2
White 70.6
Gold 68.2
Ladies Gold 73.7
Ladies Red 69.9

COURTESY OF DATAW ISLAND

"When the course . . . isn't bordered on both sides by trees, the view includes various degrees of tidewater area, populated by gull, egret, pelican, fish and alligator. When you add a human toting a bundle of sticks, it doesn't change the scene that much."

I wish I'd written that description of the Cotton Dike Course on Dataw Island, but I didn't. Al Ludwich of the *Augusta Chronicle* did. He captured the exact feeling you get when you play this beautiful and isolated course not too many miles from the old port city of Beaufort

Nearly 140 years ago, the Sams brothers of Beaufort attempted to increase Dataw Island's arable land by building a system of dikes out from the shore. The idea was to trap water and earth and build up the land through the gradual process of siltation in order to increase the production of the staple crop of the period, sea-island cotton. Evidence of the dikes and the old channels to the cotton port is still with us today.

These remaining bits of history are what inspired the Cotton Dike Course's name.

Tom Fazio, the builder of the course, said, "From the time you enter the security gate you get a feeling of quality. There's a character, a style here that is outstanding even before you get to the 1st tee."

I've played the course several times, and I'm here to say that each time it's different and each time it's a joy. The 17th and 18th are incredible finishing holes, and every time I've come in on the 18th and seen the sun setting on the beautiful clubhouse, I've thought about going into the real-estate office and telling anyone there who will listen that I give up—I'm buying.

On my last visit, I had a chance to play a hole with one of the great golf architects in the business, Arthur Hills, who has just completed nine holes on the new Morgan Creek Course here, bringing the total on Dataw Island to twenty-seven. Nine more holes will be built on the Mor-

HOLE NUMBER	1	2	3	4	5	6	7	8	9	OUT	10	11	12	13	14	15	16	17	18	IN	TOT	HCP	NET
BLUE TEES	407	379	185	537	467 441	451	188	435	557	3606 3580	310	171	492	344	179	406	532	354	431	3219	6825 6799		
WHITE TEES	379	359	174	513	389	412	174	405	512	3317	299	149	485	297	160	387	474	327	390	2968	6285		
GOLD TEES	368	344	157	497	366	391	139	363	458	3083	262	124	471	285	122	352	462	317	346	2741	5824		
HANDICAP	11	13	17	5	9	7	15	1	3		16	18	8	12	14	2	6	10	4				
PAR	4	4	3	5	4	4	3	4	5	36	4	3	5	4	3	4	5	4	4	36	72		
RED TEES	317	323	129	434	306	343	107	313	418	2690	234	112	394	256	102	309	408	286	326	2427	5117		
HANDICAP	11	9	15	1	13	5	17	7	3		14	18	10	12	16	2	6	8	4				

PHOTOGRAPH BY FLIP CHALFONT
COURTESY OF DATAW ISLAND

gan Creek Course in the very near future. In the meantime, Dataw Island offers some beautiful and challenging holes set in what might very well be the most spectacular land in the Low Country.

The Dataw Island courses are strictly private, for members and property owners only. But if you're in the market for the ideal place to live, I'd suggest playing here and *then* looking at the houses. If the golf and the homesites don't convince you that this is the place to play eighteen a day from here on out, maybe bowling is your game.

Country Club at Edisto

FAIRFIELD'S COUNTRY CLUB AT EDISTO

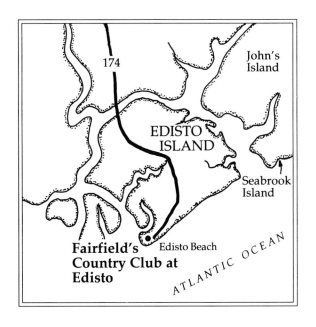

174

John's Island

EDISTO ISLAND

Seabrook Island

Fairfield's Country Club at Edisto

Edisto Beach

ATLANTIC OCEAN

1 King Cotton Road
Box 27
Edisto Island, South Carolina 29438
803-869-2561

Public

Tom Jackson, designer

Course Ratings

Blue 69.5
White M-67.8   L-72.4
Red 70.3

COURTESY OF FAIRFIELD'S COUNTRY CLUB AT EDISTO

While preferential tee times are given to the landowners at Fairfield's Country Club at Edisto, the public is more than welcome. In fact, they are so welcome that the green fees and cart rentals are the lowest in the entire area. Normally, anything that sounds this good has some catch at the bottom of the page, but there's no catch here. Fairfield is a first-class course. The greenskeepers trim the Bermuda fairways so low they look like bent grass, and the greens stay in great shape. I've played the course three times and I don't remember ever having a poor lie in the fairway.

As regards facilities and amenities, you can call the restaurant at the clubhouse from the 8th tee and order anything from soup and chicken wings to barbecue and cold beer. A menu is posted on the tee marker. After you hole out on the 9th, you can eat on the veranda overlooking the 1st and the 10th. Then you can play the 10th.

The 10th. Now there's a hole where you have to be careful. The tee is elevated some thirty or forty feet, and you have to thread your shot between two ponds and a giant oak that spreads out from the woods on the right. It's not the only oak that comes into play on the course. Back on the 5th, a par-5, there is a beauty right smack in the middle of the fairway about ninety yards from the pin. You have to go around it or over it. Some wag once said that a tree is 90 percent air. That doesn't apply to the live oaks down here, or the palmettos and the magnolias either. Your best bet on the 5th is to play it short and then take a 6- or 7-iron over it.

Fairfield is shorter than most courses, only 6,312 from the blues and 6,016 from the whites. But when you realize that there are fourteen holes where water comes into play and a total of fifty-seven sand bunkers, you'll understand just how hard a short course can be. The par-3 6th is an island hole, with the tee on another island. Despite the water and the bunkers, I always play the course from the blues. There isn't much difference in length, and the higher elevation gives you a much better view of the trouble that lies ahead.

HOLE NUMBER	1	2	3	4	5	6	7	8	9	OUT	10	11	12	13	14	15	16	17	18	IN	TOT	HCP	NET
BLUE	495	355	162	371	490	155	393	335	350	3106	434	375	138	325	384	380	175	370	525	3206	6312		
WHITE	482	340	135	360	476	128/101	380	322	340	2963	410	365	127	318	350	365	155	350	513	3053	6016		
MEN'S HDCP.	3	13	17	11	5	15	1	7	9		2	16	18	12	6	8	14	10	4				
PAR	5	4	3	4	5	3	4	4	4	36	4/5	4	3	4	4	4	3	4	5	35/36	71/72		
RED	463	318	113	330	458	70	322	298	322	2694	388	343	114	300	276	340	136	330	491	2718	5412		
LADIES' HDCP.	4	14	16	10	2	18	8	6	12		3	9	17	13	5	7	15	11	1				

Edisto Island, with over seven miles of uninterrupted beach, has managed to keep its landscape, skyline, and ecology about the way it was twenty or thirty years ago. For me, it's still one of the real jewels on the South Carolina coast. It's also one of the best areas in the entire country for collecting fossils on the beach.

At the north end of the beach is Edisto State Park. While it's small, the campground is one of the prettiest in the state. Many of the sites are set on small hills up under the live oaks, looking out on the ocean only a few yards away. The campground is equipped with electrical and water hookups, barbecue pits, and a place to shower. A grocery store is only a block away. For a golfing weekend with the family or a foursome of friends that won't cost you an arm and a leg, Edisto State Park is the place to stay.

And after you play Fairfield, spend an evening at the clubhouse restaurant, where the main attraction is a glassed-in live oak tree in the middle of the room. As soon as it's dark, a string of raccoons comes tiptoeing down the big limbs for the food that the cooks serve them. I once heard a four-year-old girl who had her face pressed to the glass say, "I thought I'd see one or two raccoons. But there were fourteen in there. Fourteen! I counted them!"

Seabrook Island Resort

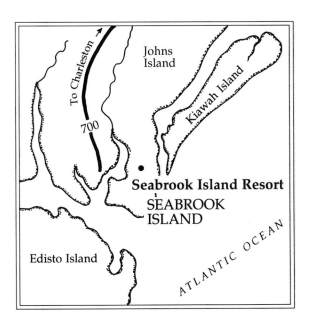

1002 Landfall Way
Johns Island, South Carolina 29455
1-800-845-2475

Semi-Private

Willard Byrd, designer—Ocean Winds
Robert Trent Jones, designer—Crooked Oaks

Course Ratings

Crooked Oaks:
Blue 73
White 70
Gold M-67, L-72
Red 69.6

Ocean Winds:
Championship 72.9
Regular 70.9
Ladies 71.4

PHOTOGRAPH BY BRIAN MORGAN COURTESY OF SEABROOK ISLAND RESORT

Seabrook Island is a twenty-two-hundred-acre island located twenty-three miles south of Charleston. On the way out to this absolute jewel of a layout, the drive goes through ten or twelve miles of the most picturesque scenery in all the Low Country. Perhaps the most famous and most exotic local landmark is the Angel Oak. You will need to make a five-hundred-yard detour to see it, but it's certainly worth the effort, for the Angel Oak is probably the largest and oldest live oak in the country, and if seen in a certain slant of light around sunset, it will take your breath away.

Also watch for the "haint" blue and green colors that the old Gullah folks still paint on their windows and door trim in an effort to keep Dr. Death on his side of the drainage ditch. Golfers have tried the same colors to correct their "banana slices," "boomerang hooks," and "yips," with some success.

Seabrook Island Resort captures the feeling of a very fine private country club, a club with a beach, a maritime forest, continental cuisine, and one of the largest wine cellars in the Carolinas. And while dining and enjoying the leaping dolphins and the long-legged Charleston beauties riding their horses through the shallows, you can also see the lagoons and the fairways of the two great courses that make Seabrook Island so perfect.

The older course is Ocean Winds, designed by Willard Byrd, while the new one, Crooked Oaks, is one of Robert Trent Jones's finest. I have played here many times, and each time I have discovered something new and great about both of them. As a matter of fact, Dan Gleason and I won second place in the Robert Trent Jones Invitational a few years back. We led after the first round, but then someone at the bar talked us into staying up all night. Anyhow, my prize was a pair of alligator shoes that weighed in at around five pounds each. Mercifully, my Labrador finally took them away and buried them out back.

Ocean Winds Course

HOLE NUMBER	1	2	3	4	5	6	7	8	9	OUT	10	11	12	13	14	15	16	17	18	IN	TOT	HCP	NET
CHAMPIONSHIP	390	382	524	404	174	482	379	193	413	3341	384	523	190	364	312	163	483	387	402	3208	6549		
REGULAR	373	360	505	380	158	468	356	174	389	3163	350	488	167	347	285	135	439	370	381	2962	6125		
HANDICAP	13	9	5	1	15	7	11	17	3		10	4	14	12	18	16	6	2	8				
PAR	4	4	5	4	3	5	4	3	4	36	4	5	3	4	4	3	5	4	4	36	72		
LADIES	325	334	471	348	128	449	322	147	362	2886	310	450	132	323	262	82	404	343	326	2632	5518		
HANDICAP	15	9	1	7	11	5	13	17	3		12	2	14	10	16	18	4	6	8				

A great idea for the golfer who loves music would be to stay at Seabrook Island during Charleston's Spoleto Festival U.S.A. in late May. And if living can get any better than that, tell me about it. I'm in the phone book.

Crooked Oaks Course

HOLE NUMBER	1	2	3	4	5	6	7	8	9	OUT	10	11	12	13	14	15	16	17	18	IN	TOT	HCP	NET
BLUE	375	501	410	412	175	545	430	390	206	3444	410	512	398	196	405	512	168	405	430	3436	6880		
WHITE	325	475	380	385	150	515	400	364	177	3171	375	475	365	164	370	490	146	365	401	3151	6322		
GOLD	300	430	350	365	125	490	380	321	140	2901	318	425	340	140	325	450	125	336	375	2834	5735		
HANDICAP	13	1	9	3	17	7	5	11	15		2	6	12	16	10	8	18	14	4				
PAR	4	5	4	4	3	5	4	4	3	36	4	5	4	3	4	5	3	4	4	36	72		
RED	258	395	337	325	115	430	350	295	135	2640	310	400	320	125	285	425	107	315	305	2592	5232		
HANDICAP	13	1	9	7	17	3	5	11	15		2	6	10	16	12	4	18	14	8				

Kiawah Island

OSPREY POINT GOLF CLUB

To Charleston

700

John's
Island

KIAWAH
ISLAND

Rockville

Seabrook
Island

ATLANTIC OCEAN

Edisto Island

P.O. Box 12357
Charleston, South Carolina 29412
803-768-2121

Semi-Private

Tom Fazio, designer

Course Ratings

Blue 71.8
White 68.8
Red 69.4

1ST HOLE

COURTESY OF KIAWAH ISLAND RESORT

Along with being the birthplace of Rhett Butler, Charleston has been home to a wide array of pirates, poets, and politicians. One of the local features that's been attracting visitors since the 1970s is Kiawah Island, a barrier island only twenty miles away.

In 1974, Kiawah Island was bought by the Kuwait Investment Company. Planners, recognizing the delicate ecological balance of the island, spent a total of $1.3 million to find out exactly how they should plan and build. So successful were the research and the resulting program that the American Society of Landscape Architects gave the company its National Merit Award for ecological planning. On June 29, 1988, five Charlestonians—Charles P. Darby III, Patrick W. McKinney, Leonard L. Long, Jr., Charles Way, Jr., and Frank W. Brumley—bought the island back from the Kuwaitis. To quote Frank W. Brumley, "Kiawah is a treasure. . . . We are working from an excellent foundation, but the best is yet to come."

With three great courses and a fourth being built for the upcoming Ryder Cup matches, Kiawah Island has become one of the great golf centers in the country. And when you add in the ten miles of undisturbed beach (rated as some of the finest in the country), the beachfront accommodations, and the island's proximity to Charleston, you are talking about a one-of-a-kind layout that could only be built in the Low Country of South Carolina.

The Osprey Point Golf Club layout is Tom Fazio at his best. From the back tees the course measures 6,678, and from the middle it's 5,968. But don't let the 5,968 lull you into thinking it's easy. Every shot here must be planned. Though the layout was completed in 1986, the owners decided to let it mature for two years before they opened it. There are four natural lakes on the course, and water comes into play on fifteen holes. Fazio has placed special emphasis on the use of moguls and mounds around the greens.

I've played the course twice. Both times, I was

HOLE NUMBER	1	2	3	4	5	6	7	8	9	OUT	10	11	12	13	14	15	16	17	18	IN	TOT	HCP	NET
BLUE	367	485	165	418	400	201	328	547	453	3364	422	205	520	350	318	165	392	398	544	3314	6678		
BLUE HANDICAP	13	17	9	3	5	7	15	11	1		6	12	14	16	10	18	8	4	2				
WHITE	331	475	149	375	366	171	295	502	397	3061	385	148	489	299	273	124	341	360	488	2907	5968		
MEN'S HANDICAP	11	13	15	5	9	7	17	3	1		2	8	12	14	18	16	10	6	4				
RED	297	403	113	342	309	142	259	440	326	2631	354	82	453	250	223	81	307	332	409	2491	5122		
RED HANDICAP	8	10	18	2	12	16	14	4	6		1	15	3	11	13	17	7	5	9				
PAR	4	5	3	4	4	3	4	5	4	36	4	3	5	4	4	3	4	4	5	36	72		

amazed at the superb conditions and the incredible range of ideas Fazio brought to this wonderful layout. I was in the high 80s each time, yet all the while I knew if I kept out of trouble, I could get into the 70s. But the trouble was there and I found it, and you know the rest.

18TH HOLE

COURTESY OF KIAWAH ISLAND RESORT

Kiawah Island®

TURTLE POINT GOLF CLUB

To Charleston

700

John's
Island

KIAWAH
ISLAND

Rockville

Seabrook
Island

ATLANTIC OCEAN

Edisto Island

P.O. Box 12357
Charleston, South Carolina 29412
803-768-2121

Semi-Private

Jack Nicklaus, designer

Course Ratings

Blue 73.5
White 70.5
Red 69.8

15TH HOLE

COURTESY OF KIAWAH ISLAND RESORT

Walking along Kiawah Island's five miles of beach, which run past Jack Nicklaus's Turtle Point Golf Course and then past Tom Fazio's Osprey Point, you could easily imagine yourself to be one of the islands off the coast of New Zealand. But all you have to do is look twenty miles away and there is old Charleston, where you can visit the spot where DuBose Heyward and George Gershwin worked on *Porgy and Bess,* or stand on the balcony of the Mills House, from which Robert E. Lee watched the old town burn.

The Jack Nicklaus layout here at Kiawah Island has been the site of a long series of amateur and professional tournaments that stretches back to Turtle Point's opening in 1981. With its 6,919 yards from the back tees, its sand traps, its bunkers, and its water hazards, the course presents a challenge you won't soon forget. The 14th, 15th, and 16th are probably the finest seaside holes in the country. They are certainly the most photogenic. The holes run right along the beach, and a hook will land you right out there with the sandpipers and the driftwood. On the other hand, with the ocean breeze coming in off the Atlantic, a high hook has an outside chance of coming back into play. I said *outside.*

Charles Way, Jr., one of the new owners of Kiawah Island, says he isn't planning to move a single sea oat or a single land-crab hole on this beachfront beauty. If he did, he would run into all kinds of trouble, for a lot of us think that what Jack Nicklaus pulled off here is his best effort yet. Of the three courses on the island, Turtle Point is the hardest because it demands the same level of concentration that Nicklaus devotes to his own game.

With three holes running along the beach and a hook getting you into nothing but sand and sea, I'd suggest a soft right hand and a cautious game off the tee. If you can stay in the middle and putt on the big greens, you can score here. But once again, you can't hook and you must putt. As a master of the fast hands and the boomerang hook, I got in more trouble at Turtle

HOLE NUMBER	1	2	3	4	5	6	7	8	9	OUT	10	11	12	13	14	15	16	17	18	IN	TOT	HCP	NET
BLUE	384	550	391	202	511	371	186	434	420	3449	520	399	443	515	168	438	173	385	429	3470	6919		
BLUE HANDICAP	13	3	11	15	7	9	17	1	5		10	12	6	8	14	2	16	18	4				
WHITE	365/338	522/494	365/335	171/152	488	289	153	405/376	382/348	3140/2973	488	367/344	420/398	483	143	407/371	153/133	325/283	398	3184/3041	6324/6014		
WHITE HANDICAP	11	3	9	17	7	13	15	1	5		10	12	4	8	16	6	14	18	2				
RED	282	436	304	134	440	250	126	344	318	2634	435	317	358	399	116	312	101	252	361	2651	5285		
RED HANDICAP	11	1	9	17	3	13	15	7	5		6	8	10	4	16	12	18	14	2				
PAR	4	5	4	3	5	4	3	4	4	36	5	4	4	5	3	4	3	4	4	36	72		

Point than I did at any other place on the island except the bar at the Kiawah Island Inn.

Down the beach from Turtle Point, Pete Dye is now building the course that will host the next Ryder Cup matches. It may very well prove to be the best course on the eastern seaboard. Ten holes—count them, ten—will run along the ocean, and the layout will look a great deal like the windswept links of the old Portmarnock course outside Dublin.

15TH HOLE

COURTESY OF KIAWAH ISLAND RESORT

Wild Dunes®

Charleston's island resort.

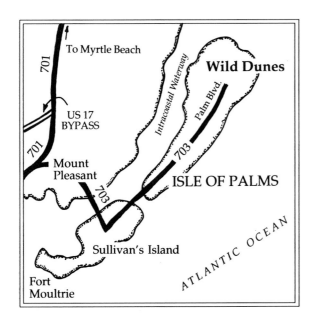

To Myrtle Beach

701

US 17 BYPASS

701

Intracoastal Waterway

Wild Dunes

Palm Blvd.

703

Mount Pleasant

703

ISLE OF PALMS

Sullivan's Island

ATLANTIC OCEAN

Fort Moultrie

P.O. Box 1410
Charleston, South Carolina 29402-1410
803-886-6000

Semi-Private

Tom Fazio, designer

WILD DUNES LINKS
ISLE OF PALMS, SOUTH CAROLINA

Golf Digest has called the Links, one of the two courses at Wild Dunes, "the ultimate in seaside golf in America." And *Golf* magazine has chosen Wild Dunes as one of the top resorts in the world. Both assessments are correct, for if there is any setting as beautiful as this seaside gem only a few miles outside Charleston, I'm not familiar with it.

If you play here on a day with little or no wind, play from the blues. The course is stunning from the back-tee elevations, and you will see why this is one of the most-photographed layouts on the seaboard.

One reason the Links is so different from other courses is the old dunes that roll along under the fairways and the greens. When the sun is setting, the rolling landscape picks up the yellows and reds, but don't let the beauty keep you from planning your shots as carefully as you know how, because everything here is deceiving. At first, you'll think it's easy. And then you'll realize that almost every shot is uphill or downhill or side-hill. In other words, you'd better not try playing in tennis shoes. You will need all the help you can get from your spikes.

I remember one round when I counted nine fairway shots in a row that were side-hillers. With my built-in hook, I had to practically take my right hand off the club to keep from hooking. And when you hook you might as well hit a provisional, because you're either in the water or out of bounds or on the beach.

After I played here twice, I finally learned my lesson, and I'm now going to pass it on to you. Check your driver in at the hotel or lock it in your car or give it to the pro. Under no circumstances should you take it out on the course. You will need all the straight balls you can get, because a twenty-yard hook or a twenty-yard fade is a disaster.

I walked over the Links about two weeks after Hurricane Hugo barreled through the area. Most of the houses situated alongside the course were either wiped out or severely damaged. It was a

Links Course

HOLE NUMBER	1	2	3	4	5	6	7	8	9	OUT	10	11	12	13	14	15	16	17	18	IN	TOT	NET
BLUE TEES	501	370	435	175	505	421	359	203	451	3420	331	380	192	427	489	426	175	405	532	3357	6777	
WHITE TEES	474	332	390	149	472	385	343	180	375	3100	293	355	169	387	477	375	145	370	510	3081	6181	
PAR	5	4	4	3	5	4	4	3	4	36	4	4	3	4	5	4	3	4	5	36	72	
RED TEES	388	268	315	98	408	260	252	113	326	2428	227	287	118	330	396	269	100	310	392	2429	4857	

WILD DUNES HARBOR COURSE
ISLE OF PALMS, SOUTH CAROLINA

terrible sight, and one that Charleston and the Low Country will never forget. The 17th and 18th were thought to be completely lost. Fortunately, the Corps of Engineers and Tom Fazio have since put their heads together and repaired the damage. The corps built back the dunes that Hugo swept away, and Fazio did the needed rebuilding and resodding. Today, the course is back in great shape and is once again near the top of everyone's list of favorites.

Harbor Course

HOLE NUMBER	1	2	3	4	5	6	7	8	9	OUT	10	11	12	13	14	15	16	17	18	IN	TOT	NET
BLUE TEES	495	437	155	472	200	392	183	570	550	3454	320	140	410	165	494	361	175	464	419	2948	6402	
WHITE TEES	485	421	145	426	175	345	165	545	491	3198	290	130	360	143	479	348	165	416	410	2741	5939	
PAR	5	4	3	4	3	4	3	5	5	36	4	3	4	3	5	4	3	4	4	34	70	
RED TEES	413	342	105	344	133	282	125	471	356	2571	258	110	305	100	375	276	118	317	321	2180	4751	

DeBordieu

701   17

DeBordieu

GEORGETOWN

18

Winyah Bay

ATLANTIC OCEAN

P.O. Box 1746
Georgetown, South Carolina 29442
1-800-476-7070

Private

Pete Dye and P. B. Dye, designers

Course Ratings

Blue 74.7
White 72.2
Gold 70.1
Green 73.5
Red 70.1

9TH HOLE

PHOTOGRAPH BY BRIAN MORGAN COURTESY OF DEBORDIEU

DeBordieu (Debbie-do) is a Pete and P. B. Dye layout with the unmistakable signature of Pete Dye all over it. Pete builds his courses for members and members only and doesn't concern himself with where the pros hit from and where they land. He often hides the back tees so members won't have to ride or walk by and see where the pros' tees are located. Pete, whose favorite course is Royal Dornoch in the north of Scotland, has given DeBordieu a definite Scottish-links look. He said, "The hills and dunes created at DeBordieu make the course play more like a Scottish layout than a typical American course."

While DeBordieu looks and plays like a Scottish course, it offers something the Scots don't have—water. Only two holes on the course *don't* have water, namely, the 11th and the 15th. In other words, on sixteen holes you are either playing left of it, right of it, or over it. I've played the course five times now, and if it's blue and it's on the left side of the fairway, I've been in it. But

regardless of its difficulty, DeBordieu is a lush course spread over one of the most beautiful vistas in the South. And also unlike Scottish courses, DeBordieu runs through a beautiful pine and hardwood forest.

A new clubhouse has just been opened here, and the word is that it crossed the finish line at something over $4 million. When golfers in the Low Country do something, they do it right. Dining facilities include a ninety-seat restaurant and a two-hundred-seat banquet room on the top floor, with a view of every egret, pelican, osprey, and blue heron in the area. I've seen five or six pileated woodpeckers from the course, and one night while staying at DeBordieu, I actually saw three wild hogs walking along the drainage ditch as if they were heading for the Magic Mart. Another night, I saw a possum share a plate of cheese nachos with a family of four raccoons. And the deer are everywhere.

The surprising thing about DeBordieu is that

HOLE NUMBER	1	2	3	4	5	6	7	8	9	OUT	10	11	12	13	14	15	16	17	18	IN	TOT	HCP	NET
BLUE	381	377	468	170	430	568	465	212	513	3584	420	497	364	427	194	427	213	449	566	3557	7141		
WHITE	365	370	415	147	365	543	400	189	455	3249	392	467	335	405	152	391	185	376	550	3253	6502		
GOLD	300	340	365	143	365	500	375	140	451	2979	361	457	300	392	145	350	149	376	515	3045	6024		
GREEN	290	339	355	128	360	488	356	143	439	2898	361	438	270	333	117	330	149	333	511	2842	5740		
MEN'S HCP	17	11	3	13	5	1	7	9	15		4	16	18	10	14	12	8	2	6				
PAR	4	4	4	3	4	5	4	3	5	36	4	5	4	4	3	4	3	4	5	36	72		
RED	237	298	332	106	319	432	301	117	405	2547	354	397	240	298	107	305	120	289	456	2566	5113		
WOMEN'S HCP	17	9	7	15	3	1	11	13	5		16	6	10	12	18	8	14	4	2				

it's much more than a golf course—it's a whole way of life, and much prettier than even Brian Morgan can photograph.

The pro here is Robert Moser, and since he spent his formative years as a professional in Columbia, he is one of the finest teachers in the business. If you play DeBordieu and you need anything, like a quick fix for the "yips," or a radical swing adjustment, or, say, a ten o'clock tee time at Torquebrada in the south of Spain, or four tickets to the Masters, Moser is the man to see.

Heritage Club

P.O. Box 1885
Pawleys Island, South Carolina 29585
803-237-3424

Public

Larry Young and Dan Maples, designers

Course Ratings

Tournament Gold 76.5
Blue 74.5
White 72.0
Red 71.0

18TH HOLE

PHOTOGRAPH BY TIM RIBAR COURTESY OF HERITAGE CLUB

Right on Route 17, exactly one mile south of Pawleys Island, lies the Heritage Club, and if ever a club deserved the name, this is it. Built on six hundred acres with giant magnolias, three-hundred-year-old live oaks, towering pines, freshwater lakes, and marshes on what was once an eighteenth-century rice plantation, the Heritage is one of those beauties that you see only in the movies. The first impression you get is that you've made a wrong turn and wandered into a very private, very exclusive club. You might even find yourself looking around for the Dobermans. But you can relax, because the Heritage is wide open to anyone with a set of sticks.

I've played the course twice: once from the blues and once from the championship golds. Why I played from the golds I'll never know. Anyhow, I won't be doing it again. Water comes into play on nine holes, and with sand bunkers spotting the fairways out where the hooks and the fades land, this is one difficult course.

From the blues it's a perfect course, and I had an 80 by keeping down the middle off the tee. There's nothing like a good score to make you appreciate the subtle beauties of a course, and if I had to do it, I could come up with the configuration of the clouds in what, that day, was a perfect sky. In short, I will return to the Heritage blues again and again.

A good tip on the blues is to put away your driver and tee off with a 3-wood. The ten to twenty yards you lose will be more than offset by the good position you will be in for your second shot. And the second shot here is the important one. Another tip is not to be afraid of a few run-up shots. The course is in such good shape around the greens that a run-up will bounce straight and run true. On the other hand, if you're hitting your wedges crisply, the greens will not only hold a fifty- or sixty-yarder, they'll help you back it up. With either shot, try to keep below the flag; this is one course where you don't want to be looking at too many down-hill putts.

HOLE NUMBER	1	2	3	4	5	6	7	8	9	FRONT	10	11	12	13	14	15	16	17	18	BACK	TOT	HCP	NET
GOLD TEES	410	570	440	440	410	205	430	165	370	3440	610	170	365	235	440	460	410	440	530	3660	7100		
BLUE TEES	380	540	410	415	395	185	400	155	350	3230	520	140	340	200	400	440	380	415	510	3345	6575		
WHITE TEES	360	510	380	345	370	165	370	145	330	2975	500	125	315	175	350	420	365	385	490	3125	6100		
MEN'S HCP.	7	11	3	1	15	13	5	17	9		10	18	16	8	4	2	14	6	12				
PAR	4	5	4	4	4	3	4	3	4	35	5	3	4	3	4	4	4	4	5	36	71		
RED TEES	300	475	340	320	325	140	310	135	190	2535	475	100	275	110	340	340	350	330	470	2790	5325		
LADIES' HCP.	11	1	3	7	5	17	9	15	13		6	18	16	14	2	12	8	10	4				

PHOTOGRAPH BY TIM RIBAR
COURTESY OF HERITAGE CLUB

Though the greens undulate, they are well kept and true, and the fringes and collars are in excellent shape. Overall, the Heritage is one of the best-maintained public courses in the business. And speaking of bests, the clubhouse is just that. Situated at the end of a remarkable stand of live oaks draped in Spanish moss, and highlighted by camellias, dogwood, and azaleas, it's perfect for this stunning club. If Hollywood were reshooting *Gone With the Wind* and needed a shot of Scarlett and Rhett sitting at a fountain in front of an antebellum mansion, the Heritage would be the ideal location.

PAWLEYS PLANTATION
GOLF & COUNTRY CLUB

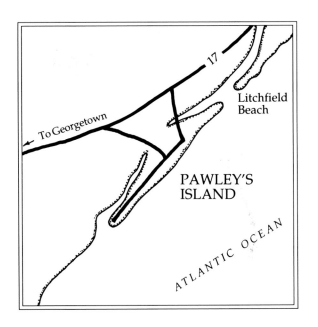

P.O. Box 2070
Highway 17 South
Pawleys Island, South Carolina 29585
803-237-8497

Semi-Private

Jack Nicklaus, designer

Course Ratings

Gold 74.3
Blue 72.5
White 69.8
Red 73.0

14TH HOLE

PHOTOGRAPH BY BRIAN MORGAN COURTESY OF PAWLEYS PLANTATION GOLF AND COUNTRY CLUB

Jack Nickalus not only built the course here at Pawleys Plantation Golf and Country Club, he bought a house back among the tall trees and the Spanish moss. And if he's as smart as he's supposed to be, he'll stay forever. When I played here the last time with my Nicklaus clubs and my Nicklaus shoes, shirt, bag, socks, and balls, I had a good round. As a matter of fact, I was hitting them so long and so straight that I imagined Big Jack was not only watching me and approving, but waiting on the next tee to join me. It's a good thing he didn't, because my hook came back and there were no more pars.

So while I didn't get to play with Jack, it's nice knowing he has a house back here. I grew up in the Low Country swimming in the creeks, freezing in the duck blinds, and hanging around the piers. I had my first car and my first cigarette here, and I played one of my first rounds of golf not too far up the road. I can remeber when I was in the third grade how the live oaks looked more like dinosaurs than did dinosaurs them-

selves, and how I figured that if the pterodactyls ever returned, this is where they would roost and raise their families.

When I played at Pawleys Plantation last, I realized that while some things change, most things down in the Low Country don't. The great blue heron is as solitary as he's ever been, and the sandpipers still go clicking along the shallows eating their microscopic meals. The osprey faithfully builds her nest in the most unlikely of places, and the pelicans look like they will always look—like spectacular drunks rowing their way home with the shrimp boats and the dying sun.

The course at Pawleys Plantation plays over marshland and tidewater, and a stray ball is often a lost ball. But the fairways are wide, and if you keep the ball in play you'll find that the greens are honest and true. If you can get down in two from thirty or forty feet, you won't be ashamed of your score.

Bluebird boxes are posted at the 150-yard

HOLE NUMBER	1	2	3	4	5	6	7	8	9	OUT	10	11	12	13	14	15	16	17	18	IN	TOT	HCP	NET
GOLDEN BEAR	511	461	194	543	390	432	172	452	416	3571	361	563	382	145	525	391	444	201	443	3455	7026		
BLUE HERON	495	441	170	498	371	391	151	419	387	3323	330	548	345	115	495	374	423	167	402	3195	6522		
WHITE EGRET	484	408	162	468	353	382	131	387	358	3133	301	542	331	69	471	364	405	139	372	2994	6127		
HANDICAP	17	1	11	13	5	7	15	3	9		12	16	18	6	8	14	2	10	4				
PAR	5	4	3	5	4	4	3	4	4	36	4	5	4	3	5	4	4	3	4	36	72		
RED TAIL HAWK	426	354	127	450	322	367	112	361	351	2870	278	442	309	40	446	351	360	122	342	2690	5560		

markers, and from every indication the birds have not only taken up residence, but a third and fourth generation will soon be with us.

Caution: unless you're over 240 off the tee and can kill a 1-iron, I'd stay as far away as possible from the gold tees and their 7,026 yards, 74.3 rating, and 132 slope reading. That is, unless you like true pain.

WACHESAW PLANTATION CLUB

P.O. Box 570
Murrells Inlet, South Carolina 29576
803-357-1500

Private

Tom Fazio, architect

Course Ratings

Championship 73.3
Men 71.2
Ladies 68.2

PHOTOGRAPH BY BRIAN MORGAN COURTESY OF WACHESAW PLANTATION

Twenty minutes south of the center of Myrtle Beach is the Wachesaw Plantation Club, a historic river-front plantation that was recently turned into a private golf community. With its stunning clubhouse, which is a replica of the eighteenth-century Dean Hall Plantation home, the club and the course are second to none in the country. Created by Tom Fazio, the course has rolling fairways lined by lovegrass knolls and grass bunkers. The Wachesaw Club is so unlike any of Fazio's other courses that he has tagged this design "the Wachesaw look." The course has been rated number one on the Grand Strand by *Golf Digest* and is fast moving up on all the charts.

I've played the course five or six times, and I love it. My favorite hole is hard to pick, but I guess if pressed I would have to say the 18th. The first and second shots must be played along the right side to avoid the lake that borders the left. From there, the third must be perfect, because the green is narrow and water is only a few yards away. While the hole finishes on the bluffs over the Waccamaw River and is a photographer's dream come true, it is almost too hard to be fair. Why then do I like it? Simple. One time when I played it, my first and second shots were down the right side of the middle. My third was on the pin. I had a birdie for a net eagle. Why else does anyone really like a hole?

There's a story floating around about how, on the 13th at Congressional, Tip O'Neill hit a sand shot out of a bunker stiff to the pin and holed it for a birdie. But two holes later, it took him four strokes to get out of the sand on the 15th. Later, when a reporter asked him to talk about how unfair the trap on the 15th was, O'Neill said, "If you don't want to talk about my shot on 13, I don't want to talk about 15."

Which I think sums it all up. The charm and the mystery that surround golf will always be those spectacular, isolated, and never-to-be-repeated moments.

Anyhow, the Wachesaw Club can only be played by residents and their guests. It doesn't

HOLE NUMBER	1	2	3	4	5	6	7	8	9	OUT	10	11	12	13	14	15	16	17	18	IN	TOT	HCP	NET
CHAMPIONSHIP	407	426	165	475	415	455	177	537	386	3446	412	355	569	179	330	378	443	207	573	3446	6889		
MEN	368	376	125	470	384	427	159	506	345	3160	378	325	535	155	302	369	412	171	535	3182	6342		
HANDICAP	13	7	17	11	5	3	9	1	15		8	16	2	18	14	12	4	10	6				
PAR	4	4	3	5	4	4	3	5	4	36	4	4	5	3	4	4	4	3	5	36	72		
LADIES	285	293	97	377	324	371	87	414	296	2544	312	245	430	122	227	281	307	111	410	2445	4989		
HANDICAP	11	9	17	7	3	5	15	1	13		6	16	2	18	14	10	8	12	4				
PAR	4	4	3	5	4	4	3	5	4	36	4	4	5	3	4	4	4	3	5	36	72		

matter what hotel you stay in or what RV lot you park in, you can't play unless you're a member or know a member. So here's what you do. The next time you see a golfer with a Wachesaw Club emblem on a shirt or a skirt or a pair of socks, buy a round of drinks and tell him or her you can guarantee a good tee time at Cypress Point or Merion or the Old Course at St. Andrews. Then, after you write down the person's name and when he or she wants to play, mention that in the meantime, since you're in the neighborhood and you have your sticks in the car, you'd like to try the Wachesaw Club. If that doesn't work, try a full nelson, because this is one course that is an overwhelming must.

MYRTLE BEACH HILTON

Arcadian Shores
GOLF CLUB

701 Hilton Road
Myrtle Beach, South Carolina 29577
803-449-5000

Public

Rees Jones, architect

Course Ratings

Tiger 73.2
Champions 71.1
White 68.8
Red 69.9

COURTESY OF THE MYRTLE BEACH HILTON

Ten miles north of Myrtle Beach, and on property now owned by the Hilton Hotel, lies the Arcadian Shores Golf Club. Designed by one of the premier golf architects on the scene today, Rees Jones, the course combines the best of mother nature and the best of a modern golf layout. The 13th and 14th, the signature holes, cross a cypress-studded lake that looks like it's been here since the beginning of time. If you stand long enough in a certain slant of light, you'll find yourself waiting for the pterodactyls to land. These two holes are nothing short of spectacular. The tall pines, magnolias, and live oaks that frame the rest of the course create the perfect setting for the Arcadian Shores layout, which *Golf* and *Golf Digest* have placed in their top fifty year in and year out.

I've played the course four or five times over the years, and every time I was surprised by the variety of the holes, the lush setting, and the spectacular forest through which the course winds. Since the purchase by the Hilton chain,

guests at the hotel have been granted preferential tee times, but the course is open year-round to guests staying in a number of select hotels in the Myrtle Beach area.

While the idea of a hotel owning such a facility has the ring of an executive, resort-type course—or a hotel course in Switzerland with short holes, few traps, and a layout that guarantees that every high handicapper can break 90—that is not the case here. Arcadian Shores is a first-class, grade-A course with sixty-four carefully placed sand bunkers and at least six natural lakes. From the back tees, the 6,938 yards can and will stand up to the best of the pros. As a matter of cold fact, Randy Glover's course-record 68 from the tips has remained long enough for a lot of us to wonder if it will ever be broken. At the same time, this is a tight and challenging and wonderful course to play from the regulation tees.

Arcadian Shores is also one of the few courses this far south that has bent-grass greens, and

HOLE NUMBER	1	2	3	4	5	6	7	8	9	OUT	10	11	12	13	14	15	16	17	18	IN	TOT	HCP	NET
TIGER	533	205	505	404	415	417	366	187	386	3418	506	424	384	415	409	216	556	164	446	3520	6938		
CHAMPIONS	504	178	466	386	392	389	339	153	364	3171	472	394	370	393	395	196	527	141	409	3297	6468		
WHITE	475	156	463	368	368	372	324	147	346	3019	440	364	350	364	273	153	515	116	380	2955	5974		
HANDICAP	8	4	10	12	2	6	18	16	14		9	3	13	1	11	15	7	17	5				
PAR	5	3	5	4	4	4	4	3	4	36	5	4	4	4	4	3	5	3	4	36	72		
RED	415	135	418	342	348	355	296	127	307	2743	402	275	309	277	261	120	462	89	356	2551	5294		

under the expert care of the new management and the new money from the Hilton, they have never been in better shape. For a weekend of top-flight golf only a few hundred yards from your hotel room, with a guaranteed tee time, you'll have to go a long way to beat Arcadian Shores. And while you're staying at the Hilton, the concierge will arrange tee times for you at other courses in the immediate area.

THE DUNES GOLF AND BEACH CLUB

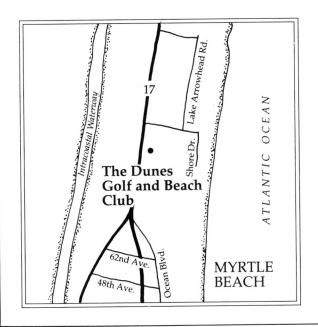

9000 North Ocean Boulevard
Myrtle Beach, South Carolina 29572
803-449-5236

Semi-Private

Robert Trent Jones, designer

Course Ratings

Gold 74.0
Blue 71.5
Red 70.0

PHOTOGRAPH BY MICHAEL SLEAR COURTESY OF BRANDON ADVERTISING

Every year, the Dunes Golf and Beach Club hosts the Golf Writers of America outing, and for three days of golf and speeches, the old Robert Trent Jones masterpiece becomes our home away from home. The so-called clambake is one week before the Masters, and it is then that writers, publishers, and editors get together to trade gossip, jokes, and jobs and in no small way decide what we're going to write about the next year. We also get to listen to spellbinding speeches from golf course superintendents about bent grass, Bermuda grass, and the latest trends in fertilizer mixes.

While we're at the Dunes, everything is free: the golf, the carts, the food, the booze, even the balls. Is it then any wonder that no civilized golf writer will say a single word against the course or the club or the bar or the facilities in the locker room? But the fact is, even if we wanted to, there would be nothing we could say that wasn't complimentary.

I've played the Dunes a dozen times, six at least with the golf writers, and I'm here to say that when you consider everything, including the driving range, the putting green, the locker room, the walls of trophies, and golf history, this is right up there with the best of the best.

The course has withstood the test of over forty years, which is no small thing. The USGA has admitted that since 1970 the ball travels 12 yards farther. What that does to the average 6,500-yard course is simply reduce it by 500 yards, which means the pros can put away their drivers and use 3-woods. Anyhow, the Dunes has held up well under the souped-up ball, the graphite shaft, square grooves, and almost any game.

Robert Trent Jones sculpted many of the holes so perfectly that they look like they have been here forever. Using an old Scottish trick, he also placed the tees and fairways in such a way that the wind hits golfers from every direction on the compass.

The Dunes is one course I have always wanted to like, but say what you will, you can't like a course where you can't break 90. Then last year I had an 86, and all the 90s vanished. Now when I

HOLE NUMBER	1	2	3	4	5	6	7	8	9	OUT	10	11	12	13	14	15	16	17	18	IN	TOT	HCP	NET
GOLD	424	422	431	508	203	436	397	535	188	3544	381	358	191	576	455	531	360	178	441	3471	7015		
GOLD HANDICAP	5	9	7	17	15	3	1	11	13		10	12	16	8	2	18	6	14	4				
BLUE	399	391	398	465	176	413	378	491	164	3275	337	325	173	526	411	495	341	162	372	3142	6417		
BLUE HANDICAP	5	9	7	17	11	1	3	15	13		8	10	12	2	4	18	14	16	6				
PAR	4	4	4	5	3	4	4	5	3	36	4	4	3	5	4	5	4	3	4	36	72		
RED	269	291	348	401	134	308	294	394	110	2549	314	290	149	440	292	429	320	137	323	2694	5243		
RED HANDICAP	13	11	3	1	15	7	9	5	17		4	10	16	2	12	14	8	18	6				

think of the Dunes, I remember the 86 and what I did on the 14th, which is on everybody's monster list. The 14th remains as scaly and fire-breathing as ever, and you can still bite off just as much as you want. Or you can bail out to the left. The 14th and the seventeen other holes around it are the reasons why *Golf* and *Golf Digest* consistently place the Dunes in the top fifty courses in the country year in and year out.

The club and clubhouse are right on the ocean, with a beautiful view of the beach. How the greenskeeper can keep the course so green and lush and true with the ocean spray and the salt in the air is one of those miracles I will never understand. In any event, the Dunes, probably the most famous course on the beach, is a must for golfing in the Carolinas, and no portfolio is complete without it. While the club is private, guests staying at a number of select hotels on the beach are allowed to play. So when you are making reservations, the first question you ask should not concern the rates or if the room is on the ocean or whether the bed comes equipped with Magic Fingers—the salesman's friend—but whether the hotel guarantees that you can play at the Dunes. If it doesn't, tell them you'll call back. Then call the desk at the Dunes and ask where you should stay.

LEGENDS

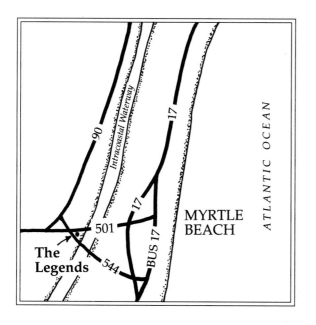

P.O. Box 65
North Myrtle Beach, South Carolina 29597
803-236-9318

Public

Tom Doak, designer

Course Ratings

Tournament 74.5
Regular 72.0
Green 71.0

PHOTOGRAPH BY MICHAEL SLEAR COURTESY OF BRANDON ADVERTISING

Larry and Judy Young, the developers who brought us Marsh Harbour and Oyster Bay, have just opened what will surely be their biggest success. It is called the Legends, and when it's completely finished, it will be a public golf facility second to none in the country.

Beginning with the premise that there are not enough public courses to absorb the increased play, the Youngs have constructed two of their three proposed courses and most of the complex. Located just off U.S. 501 four miles west of Myrtle Beach, the Tom Doak–designed courses will offer a distinctly different look.

The first course, the Heathland, has been artificially molded, at considerable expense, in the image of the early British courses, with holes reminiscent of familiar links like St. Andrews and little-known gems like Lahinch and Ballybunion in Ireland. The Heathland is a spectacular links course, and it requires a completely different game from the one you're probably used to playing.

In 1989, P. J. Carroll and Company, the sponsors of the Irish Open, invited three of us American golf writers to play in the pro-am on the day before the open. We played with Christy O'Connor, the former champion, at Portmarnock, outside Dublin. The course, built on a peninsula jutting into the Irish Sea, doesn't have a single tree or a single water hole. Very quickly I saw why—it doesn't need them because it has something else. The course has its distinctive natural terrain, which presents enough hazards, but most of all it has the wind. The Scottish have a saying, "No wind, no golf." Well, we had wind. We played into the wind on some holes and downwind on others and across the wind on the rest. It was inescapable and we were never out of it. But it didn't seem to bother O'Connor. Finally, I asked him how he kept the ball so low and stayed under it, and he said, "Laddie, you have to think low."

The reason I'm telling you this is that when I played the Heathland course at the Legends, it

Heathland Course

HOLE NUMBER	1	2	3	4	5	6	7	8	9	OUT	10	11	12	13	14	15	16	17	18	IN	TOT	NET
CHAMPIONSHIP	450	345	210	355	560	460	460	147	405	3392	435	400	165	535	385	345	450	220	410	3345	6737	
REGULAR	420	310	190	335	530	385	425	130	365	3090	405	380	150	510	350	315	430	185	375	3100	6190	
HANDICAP	3	15	13	11	5	1	9	17	7		4	6	18	12	16	14	2	10	8			
PAR	4	4	3	4	5	4	5	3	4	36	4	4	3	5	4	4	4	3	4	35	71	
LADIES	370	235	130	285	450	250	390	90	330	2530	330	325	110	475	270	270	385	120	305	2590	5120	

reminded me a great deal of Portmarnock. Once again the wind was blowing, and once again I had the same problem of keeping the ball low. There are also other problems. You have to count on the fact that you will be hitting a lot of bump-and-run shots. A high wedge in a high wind is a terrible thing to watch. It's almost as terrible as watching a 220-yard drive go out about 100 yards and then suddenly rise and then stop and then drop down out around 110. You will see a lot of that at the Heathland, but when you finish you'll be a far wiser golfer, and you will get some idea of what golf is like back in the land where it all began.

In addition to the Heathland and the two other courses—the Moorland and the Parkland—there is a state-of-the-art thirty-acre practice facility that includes the Phil Ritson Golf School and a huge hitting clock, a circular setup that allows golfers to choose their own wind conditions. And if that isn't enough, the clubhouse is modeled on the theme of a Scottish village, with a golf museum, a club maker's shop, a restaurant, a complete pro shop, and the ever-present Guinness-serving pub. Which is where, if the wind is high enough and you haven't learned how to hit low and keep low, you may be spending more time than it takes Bernhard Langer to line up a seven-footer.

PINE LAKES INTERNATIONAL COUNTRY CLUB

P.O. Box 7099
Woodside Drive
Myrtle Beach, South Carolina 29577-7099
803-449-6459

Semi-Private

Robert White, designer

Course Ratings

Championship 71.3
Regular 69.4
Ladies 71.2

PHOTOGRAPH BY MICHAEL SLEAR COURTESY OF BRANDON ADVERTISING

Pine Lakes International Country Club, affectionately called "the Granddaddy," is the oldest course on the Grand Strand. It is in the center of Myrtle Beach and is a superb layout that the club members keep in marvelous shape. Built in 1927, Pine Lakes is the course where Bobby Jones, Horton Smith, and Gene Sarazen teed up, and there are great pictures in the lobby to prove it. It is also the place where, in 1954, a group of sixty-seven executives from Time-Life came by train to play and to plan a magazine that has been with us ever since. It's called *Sports Illustrated*. The course was designed and built by Robert White of St. Andrews, Scotland, the founding father of Grand Strand golf.

Scottish heritage and Southern hospitality are a wonderful combination, and nowhere are they in evidence more strongly than at Pine Lakes— five starters dress in Scottish kilts. Out on the 10th tee, Eddie Dingle, the club chef for forty years, presides over an iron pot of his complimentary Low Country clam chowder. He serves it to every golfer at the turn. And on cool mornings, Eddie serves hot chocolate on the 1st tee. All the help at Pines Lakes is outstanding. Their motto goes: "The minute you arrive until you leave, the only time you touch your clubs is when you're hitting the ball." In other words, they meet you at your car, carry your clubs in, clean them when you are finished, and then take them back to your car.

One look at the sixty-two-room antebellum mansion as you come up the winding, magnolia-lined driveway at Pine Lakes is enough to make you wish the South had won the war. It was designed by Henry Bacon, the same man who designed the Lincoln Memorial, and it is the finest example of its kind in the area. Inside, you will find string quartets during afternoon teas and photographs on the walls that go back to the Roaring Twenties. The Rockefellers and the Vanderbilts were members at Pine Lakes, and Bobby Jones, Donald Ross, and Alister Mackenzie spent many happy days on the verandas

HOLE NUMBER	1	2	3	4	5	6	7	8	9	OUT	10	11	12	13	14	15	16	17	18	IN	TOT	HCP	NET
CHAMPIONSHIP	563	432	428	406	185	378	159	367	493	3411	344	185	495	428	355	200	379	442	370	3198	6609		
REGULAR	539	411	405	382	153	355	134	349	463	3191	319	164	475	403	328	177	363	407	349	2985	6176		
MEN'S HDCP.	9	3	1	7	15	11	13	5	17		14	16	18	2	10	12	6	4	8				
PAR	5	4	4	4	3	4	3	4	5	36	4	3	5	4	4	3	4	4	4	35	71		
LADIES'	476	355	363	308	142	294	108	313	423	2782	296	150	421	341	279	162	281	362	302	2594	5376		
LADIES' HDCP.	5	3	1	9	15	13	17	11	7		10	18	6	2	14	16	12	4	8				

looking out over the azaleas and planning the course over in Augusta that was to become the Masters. And if you visit the Masters and get a chance to sit on its veranda, which looks out through a wisteria-hung live oak, you will see the unmistakable touch of the Granddaddy.

While Pine Lakes is a private layout with a private membership, the course and its amenities are open to the guests of many of the better hotels on the beach. If I had to single out one outstanding feature of Myrtle Beach and Grand Strand golf, it would be that a golfer can check in at a hotel and have twenty courses to choose from. That fact is truly outstanding.

CAMDEN COUNTRY CLUB

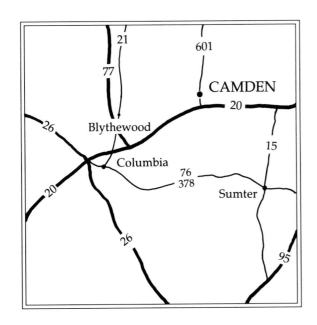

111 Knights Hill Road
Camden, South Carolina 29020
803-432-3322

Private

Walter Travis, redesigned by Donald Ross

Course Ratings

Blue 70.1
White 69.1
Red 70.2

PHOTOGRAPH BY DANNY ALLEN COURTESY OF CAMDEN COUNTRY CLUB

1 0 4

At the Camden Country Club, they don't over-seed with ryegrass for winter play. Instead, they leave the Bermuda alone, and when it goes dormant, the fairways take on the soft color of an old Brooks Brothers camel's-hair coat. Somehow the color seems to fit this venerable course. Whether you play or just stand around and watch, you begin to realize that the Camden Country Club is one of the high-water marks of golf in our country.

The course was originally laid out for the Kirkwood Hotel, a renowned two-hundred-room luxury resort that opened in 1903. Right after World War I, Walter Travis, the first American to win the British Amateur Championship, had a hand in revamping the course. Twenty years after Travis, Donald Ross came down from Pinehurst, and after redesigning everything and getting rid of the sand greens, he installed what were probably the first grass greens in South Carolina.

Today, while the old course measures only 6,236 from the blues and 5,985 from the whites, it is still one of the great layouts to play. First of all, it's fairly flat and you can walk. Second, it's cut out of a forest of tall pines, oaks, and magnolias. And third, it has those Donald Ross greens.

Ross's greens are shaped like inverted saucers. On days when they are as firm as they should be, you have to be very careful. A slightly missed shot will not only fail to stick on the green, it will roll off the other side. On the other hand, if you've got a good chipping game or you can use your Texas wedge from the fringe, you can probably beat some afficionado with a Ping square-groove beryllium wedge.

I've played the course twice from the blues, and both times I scored in the low 80s. The secret I found was to lay up short and keep my approaches below the hole. A downhill putt can be fatal. As a matter of fact, many of the greens here remind me of the 12th hole at the Masters. I

HOLE NUMBER	1	2	3	4	5	6	7	8	9	OUT	10	11	12	13	14	15	16	17	18	IN	TOT	HCP	NET
BLUE TEES	374	177	538	395	316	229	437	154	369	2989	419	372	169	483	418	419	189	399	379	3247	6236		
WHITE TEES	361	165	527	379	302	209	425	145	356	2869	404	350	157	465	403	404	177	385	371	3116	5985		
MEN'S HCP.	7	11	1	3	9	13	15	17	5		2	18	16	12	8	4	14	6	10				
MEN'S PAR	4	3	5	4	4	3	5	3	4	35	4	4	3	5	4	4	3	4	4	35	70		
RED TEES	349	125/140	443	330	263	195	385	137	302	2529/2544	352	328	145	439	322	359	165	345	328	2783	5312/5327		
LADIES' HCP.	7	13	1	3	11	5	15	17	9		6	14	18	2	12	4	16	8	10				
LADIES' PAR	4	3	5	4	4	3	5	3	4	35	4	4	3	5	4	4	3	4	4	35	70		

PHOTOGRAPH BY DANNY ALLEN
COURTESY OF CAMDEN COUNTRY CLUB

putted downhill there one time for a birdie and wound up not only off the green but in the creek.

Anyhow, today, with our long drivers, our hot balls, and our smooth fairways, a 420-yard par-4 is a drive and a wedge for a long hitter. Perhaps Donald Ross saw this coming and designed his greens with the future in mind. At Camden Country Club, his ghost is out there with you on every approach and every putt. This fine course has a great clubhouse with an enormous porch overlooking the 1st tee, the 10th tee, and the 18th green. For a small country club with few frills, this is my favorite. And one more thing: in the grill, they offer delicious chicken fried in honest grease, served right over the counter.

The Windermere Club

FOUNDED 1987

2004 Longtown Road East
Blythewood, South Carolina 29016
803-754-2071

Private

Pete Dye and P. B Dye, designers

Course Ratings

Tee I 65.9
Tee II 67.1
Tee III 69.5
Tee IV 71.7
Tee V 73.6

COURTESY OF FAIRWAYS DEVELOPMENT

Pete Dye, the man who gave the world Harbour Town, Long Cove, DeBordieu, the PGA West, and the Tournament Players Club at Sawgrass, has built a brand-new layout in Blythewood, a few miles from Columbia. It's called the Windermere Club, and I've played it twice and loved it even in the rain. First of all, it's a true gem and an absolute joy to play. Second, it's right in my own backyard.

Herbert Warren Wind, probably the best golf writer breathing, believes that Pete is without question the most imaginative and creative golf course architect in the world today. Wind will get no argument from me on that, because the courses Pete and his son P. B. have designed are a virtual all-star list of championship links. *Golf* magazine currently ranks eight Dye layouts in the top hundred courses in the world.

Pete and P. B. have built courses everywhere, and on some of the most unpromising land imaginable. In the Dominican Republic, Pete carved one of the most beautiful courses in the world out of solid coral. It was a similar story out in California, where he built the PGA West with nothing to work with but flat desert. The result was a layout already being considered the greatest golf course built in recent years.

After working with desert and coral, Pete and P. B. were stunned and delighted when they looked out over the rolling land around the big lake at Windermere. "The natural lay of the land here made our job easy," Pete said. "The course was already there, we merely needed to carve it out."

And carve it out is exactly what they did. All the holes here fit the landscape, and nowhere is there any evidence of heavy bulldozing. Like many great courses, Windermere follows the natural terrain, and when you play it you can feel it. The site itself, which has the highest elevation in the county, is covered with pines and oaks, giving it a distinctive Pinehurst look. But unlike Pinehurst, the high elevations, the severe mounds, and the countless bunkers give Wind-

HOLE NUMBER	1	2	3	4	5	6	7	8	9	OUT	10	11	12	13	14	15	16	17	18	IN	TOT	HCP	NET
TEE V	387	412	542	198	388	507	446	483	204	3567	509	410	394	207	310	461	423	158	531	3403	6970		
TEE IV	369	390	512	177	365	486	424	445	202	3370	483	382	370	181	288	434	402	138	503	3181	6551		
TEE III	348	355	483	163	337	472	383	413	187	3141	456	341	339	152	267	406	356	136	475	2928	6069		
TEE II	328	305	454	134	302	446	351	382	175	2877	431	293	322	110	245	368	336	115	442	2662	5539		
TEE I	299 261	263	426	113	263	406	332	346	130	2578 2540	412	256	293	110	216	318	305	107 88	401	2418 2399	4996 4939		
HANDICAP	13	5	9	11	17	15	7	1	3		8	12	10	14	16	2	4	18	6				
PAR	4	4	5	3	4	5	4	4	3	36	5	4	4	3	4	4	4	3	5	36	72		

ermere a look that only a Dye course could have.

Another interesting feature you won't find on many courses is the use of five different strains of grass, namely, Bermuda, bent, centipede, zoysia, and lovegrass. The result is that you can see exactly where the fairway edges the rough and where the apron rings the green by the changes in coloration.

There are five tees at Windermere—count them, five. From the back, the course comes in at 6,970 yards, and from the front, it's 4,939. The idea is that the long hitters and the pros can play from the back, while average golfers and novices can choose any of the other four. In any event, the course they play is a Pete and P. B. Dye true masterpiece set in some of the most spectacular and beautiful land in the state.

Palmetto
Golf Club

275 Berrie Road
Aiken, South Carolina 29801
803-649-2951

Private

Originally designed by Herbert Leeds
Redesigned by Alister Mackenzie

Course Ratings

Championship 71.1
White 68.8

PHOTOGRAPH BY SCOTT WEBSTER COURTESY OF PALMETTO GOLF CLUB

If the Palmetto Golf Club, located right in the center of Aiken, isn't the oldest course in the country, it's close. It's the only course I've ever run across where you can still find gutta percha balls in the rough. The gutta percha has been extinct since 1900.

In 1895, Palmetto hosted the Southern Cross Tournament, which according to my records was the first golf tournament in the country. Up over one of the six fireplaces in the old clubhouse is the winner's trophy. Palmetto is not only an old course, it's also one of the best ones I've every played. The club is all golf: no bowling or tennis or swimming, no big board showing the stock-market reports, not even food, just golf.

Twelve identical rockers sit on the porch overlooking the 18th green and the 1st tee the way they have been sitting since the clubhouse was built in 1902. And speaking of clubhouses, this is a one-of-a-kind jewel designed and built by none other than Evelyn Nesbit's lover, Stanford White. White was also the man behind the clubhouse at Shinnecock on Long Island, Madison Square Garden, and a list of other great buildings as long as your arm.

As for the course at Palmetto, it is also a one-of-a-kind masterpiece. It was built by Alister Mackenzie, the same Scotsman behind Augusta National, Royal Melbourne, and Cypress Point. The course was originally built by Herbert Lee and Jimmy Mackrell in 1892, back during the days of gutta percha balls and sand greens. In 1932, Mackenzie, fresh from working with Bobby Jones on Augusta National, crossed the Savannah River to remodel and lengthen Palmetto and replace the sand greens with Bermuda grass.

Mackenzie, a camouflage expert in World War I, believed that a course should be designed so that distances are concealed and so that the real contest is not off the tee but with iron play, approaches, and putting. A good example of that philosophy is his course at Cypress Point, which

HOLE NUMBER	1	2	3	4	5	6	7	8	9	OUT	10	11	12	13	14	15	16	17	18	IN	TOT	HCP	NET
BLUE TEES	345	329	395	334	342	361	109	356	140	2705	408	140	338	345	474	246	196	337	300	2784	5509		
STROKES	5	7	9	3	1	13	17	11	15		12	18	4	2	6	10	8	14	16				
PAR	4	4	5	4	4	5	3	4	3	36	5	3	4	4	5	4	3	4	4	36	72		

PHOTOGRAPH BY SCOTT WEBSTER
COURTESY OF PALMETTO GOLF CLUB

measures only 6,400 yards. Tom Watson says a 75 there is a great score. Palmetto is not as hard as Cypress Point, but many of Cypress Point's great characteristics are here as well. The greens at Palmetto undulate, and the fairways are so cleverly contoured that you really can't tell how far away the green is unless you've played the course at least a dozen times.

Many of the pros stop off at Palmetto for a practice round before they play in the Masters in Augusta, only a few miles away. In the pro shop at Palmetto is a 1952 picture of Ben Hogan playing with a few of the members, namely, E. W. Grace, E. P. Rodgers, and Robert Goodyear. There is also a 1984 shot of Tom Moore, the pro here, giving Ben Crenshaw some spiritual advice on putting. Crenshaw went on to win the Masters that year, and he's been coming back to see Tom Moore and play Palmetto every year since.

GREENVILLE COUNTRY CLUB

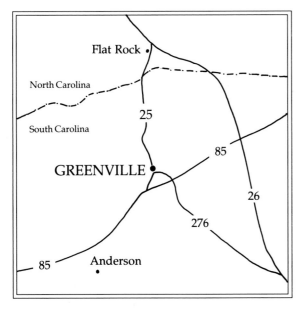

239 Bird Boulevard
Greenville, South Carolina 29605
803-232-6771

Private

Robert Trent Jones, designer

Course Ratings

White 70.0
Blue 73.0
Yellow 72.0

PHOTOGRAPH BY BOBBY ASHBURN COURTESY OF GREENVILLE COUNTRY CLUB

When I first saw the Greenville Country Club's Chanticleer Course—the club's other course is Riverside, just a few miles away—I thought I was in Pennsylvania or the hills of upstate New York. I had no idea that a course in the "hard lard belt" of South Carolina could have so many hills. The 6,668 yards from the back tees and the 6,149 from the whites play at least 400 yards longer. On the many uphill holes, there is almost no roll, and I imagine on wet days there must be a lot of plugged lies. On the other hand, the downhill holes are very, very difficult. Unless a shot is placed almost perfectly, the ball will roll off into the rough. Or if you hit it too long, you will find yourself looking at a downhill lie to a trapped green a full 3- or 4-iron away.

When I played the course, I thought I'd hit from the blues. But when I saw the 73 USGA rating and the hills that lay before me and the mountains in the distance that I knew would break the putts, I eased up to the whites. That was probably the only smart thing I did all day.

The only tips that I can pass along on Chanticleer are to place your tee shots as carefully as you can and to remember when you are putting that Robert Trent Jones tucked his greens into the foothills of the Blue Ridge Mountains, so you should allow plenty for the break. Oh, and one more. Try and get the pro to let you start your round from the 10th, which is an easy eighteen handicap. The 1st hole is a very, very tough, 412-yard one handicap.

While the Greenville Country Club was founded in 1905, the course, one of Robert Trent Jones's best, wasn't built until 1949. Overall, Chanticleer is an unbeatable combination of natural beauty and lush holes that you will long remember. And if you're not playing too well—which was what I was doing the day I played—you can take in the towering pines, the hardwoods, and the dogwoods. There is also a string of spring-fed lakes that seem to be full of bass and bream. And you can watch for deer and raccoons and an occasional lost possum.

HOLE NUMBER	1	2	3	4	5	6	7	8	9	OUT	10	11	12	13	14	15	16	17	18	IN	TOT	HCP	NET
BLUE	427	171	534	175	429	368	511	378	396	3389	365	430	391	374	169	543	172	497	338	3279	6668		
WHITE	412	140	498	147	396	352	466	345	357	3113	330	402	370	347	138	502	162	468	317	3036	6149		
MEN'S HDCP.	1	17	7	15	3	13	11	9	5		18	2	4	14	16	6	10	8	12				
PAR	4	3	5	3	4	4	5	4	4	36	4	4	4	4	3	5	3	5	4	36	72		
YELLOW	322	109	448	100	355	325	430	311	323	2723	287	361	300	322	114	453	151	433	274	2695	5418		
WOMEN'S HDCP.	11	15	1	17	9	13	3	5	7		14	6	10	12	16	2	18	4	8				

I say *you* can do this because I can't. When I'm playing as badly as I did at Chanticleer, all I can see are impossible shots in front of me, while I'm simultaneously reliving every microsecond of the sorry shots I've left behind.

But if you're playing well and keeping it down the middle, you can score. I didn't stay down the middle, and if it hadn't been for some inspired wedge shots and clever run-ups, I wouldn't have broken 95. As it was, I had an 89, which I decided I could live with. It was a warm, dry day with no wind. I imagine that on a wet, cold one with some wind, any wind, this could be one of the toughest private courses in the Southeast. But then maybe that's why *Golf Digest* and *Golf* keep on keeping Chanticleer in the top fifty in the country.

I'd say that Chanticleer is a perfect members' course, because it's one of those difficult layouts where the more you play and the more you know, the better you score. I'd also say that a twelve-handicap guest from Big Eight country, say, Kansas or Nebraska, would be lucky to come in under 100.

North Carolina

Cullasaja Club

An Arvida Community

Highway 64
Highlands, North Carolina 28741
704-526-3531

Private

Arnold Palmer, designer

Course Ratings

Back/Gold 72.1
Middle/Blue 70.2
Senior/Green 67.3
Ladies/Red 68.2

10TH FAIRWAY

COURTESY OF CULLASAJA CLUB

Some golf writer who is no longer with us once described Tommy Armour as hitting a ball with a motion that looked not unlike that of flicking a wafer off an altar cloth. I've never quite been able to visualize that, but I do know that if it's possible, the bent-grass fairways at the Cullasaja Club are where it could be done. I've never seen prettier or friendlier lies. I mean, you could step on the ball and still have a good lie. And the greens are as good as the fairways. In short, the Cullasaja Club is a great mountain course and one we should all try to play.

Arvida, the company that developed Boca West, Longboat Key, and the Tournament Players Club at Sawgrass, is in charge, and it has done a remarkable job up here in Highlands, elevation 4,118 feet. Highlands is one of the highest incorporated towns east of the Rockies, and surely one of the most attractive.

Activities in the area surrounding Highlands and the Cullasaja Club are hiking on the Appalachian Trail, rafting on the Chattooga and Nantahala rivers, and camping and enjoying breathtaking mountain views in four national forests. But all that is nothing compared to the lush golf course that Arnold Palmer designed, laid out, and built.

I played the Cullasaja Club in the cold and the rain. Despite the conditions, I can honestly report that the course is a beauty and that a few weeks after Groundhog Day I'll be back with my sticks among the dogwoods and the azaleas.

The 5th is the first of two unforgettable holes here. You tee off from an elevated tee, and the hang time for the ball seems like it's over a minute. The green setting is the most spectacular on the course. A beautiful waterfall spills over huge boulders right behind the green. It's a memorable hole, probably the most scenic on the course. The cascading waterfall is the beginning of the Cullasaja River, which runs through five of the front nine holes. Lake Ravenel winds through the back nine.

The 12th, the other great hole, will give you a

HOLE NUMBER	1	2	3	4	5	6	7	8	9	OUT	10	11	12	13	14	15	16	17	18	IN	TOT	NET
GOLD	404	510	148	401	436	480	186	348	370	3283	404	365	410	525	184	531	332	201	416	3368	6651	
BLUE	366 352	485	137	385 336	418	459	167	319	347 317	3083 2990	384 365	347	368	496	167	508	312	185	390	3157 3138	6240 6128	
GREEN	318	428	111	298	381	420	146	301	275	2678	338	310	327	484	159	471	290	179	368	2926	5604	
RED	281	393	101	271	342	388	121	258	233	2388	315	283	279	392	133	411	230	135	312	2388	4878	

13TH FAIRWAY

COURTESY OF CULLASAJA CLUB

chance to hit another spectacular tee shot, for here, too, the ball will hang in the air for what seems like forever. When you arrive at the landing area and look back at what you have just hit over and off of, you will be truly amazed. As you play the 12th and most of the others, you will come to realize that except at the higher elevations, the remaining holes are almost never in sight. I've always considered that the hallmark of a great layout. And this is certainly one.

WADE HAMPTON GOLF CLUB

Box 1920
Highway 107, South
Cashiers, North Carolina 28717
704-743-5465

Private

Tom Fazio, designer

Course Ratings

The Fazio Course 74.3
The Wade Hampton Course 71.2
The Founders Course 68.8
The Chimney Top Course 69.4

14TH HOLE

COURTESY OF WADE HAMPTON GOLF CLUB

Tom Fazio, who has put his trademark on such courses as Wild Dunes, Jupiter Hills, Butler National, Callawassie, and the Wachesaw Club, to name just a few, is the man behind the layout at Wade Hampton Golf Club. As far as a lot of us are concerned, this is the best of his best. Taking advantage of the spectacular scenery in Cashiers, which includes granite-faced mountains, beautiful streams, a forest of rhododendron, and enormous hardwood trees, he has created a course that will be nationally rated for a long, long time to come.

Fazio, speaking about the layout, said, "A course must harmonize with the environment and climate conditions. It should leave a pleasing impression of the total picture and not just be remembered for a few holes."

Waddy Stokes, director of golf at Wade Hampton, gave a survey to some golfers who had just completed their first round on the course. When asked which hole they liked best, the players ranked thirteen different holes as their most memorable. Stokes said, "We wanted to challenge the good player, but we weren't trying to build a U.S. Open course. After all, how many golfers are that great?"

High in the Blue Ridge Mountains, the course lies right next door to High Hampton in a valley framed by Chimneytop Mountain and Whiteside Mountain. From the back tees, it's a rugged 7,109, but it drops to 6,459 from the middle tees, which I played. Par is 72, and the championship tees have a USGA rating of 74.3.

Although the course is 3,650 feet above sea level, its high and low points are only 110 feet apart in elevation. It's an easy course to walk, and as Stokes said, "When caddies are available, two out of every three rounds are walkers."

The owners, A. William McKee of Cashiers and Ann McKee Austin of Atlanta, run a tight ship. A player showing up on the 1st tee with short shorts is sent back to the locker room to change. Another club custom I like is that all golf balls must be white. Orange, yellow, and neon

HOLE NUMBER	1	2	3	4	5	6	7	8	9	OUT	10	11	12	13	14	15	16	17	18	IN	TOT	HCP	NET
FAZIO	544	456	219	581	419	156	380	401	442	3598	564	168	317	411	405	429	489	193	535	3511	7109		
WADE HAMPTON	528	378	194	535	364	141	340	358	382	3220	536	151	306	392	381	410	417	171	475	3239	6459		
FOUNDERS	514	342	172	514	319	128	321	326	337	2973	501	135	281	374	360	391	383	137	420	2982	5955		
CHIMNEY TOP	442	297	116	439	260	109	258	287	286	2494	453	104	219	347	309	376	295	137	386	2626	5120		
HANDICAP	7	5	11	1	3	17	13	15	9		6	18	16	10	12	2	4	14	8				
PAR	5	4	3	5	4	3	4	4	4	36	5	3	4	4	4	4	4	3	5	36	72		

1ST HOLE

COURTESY OF WADE HAMPTON GOLF CLUB

pink are not only frowned upon, they are simply not allowed.

When I played it, the course was in spectacular shape, and I've never putted on better greens. The fairways feature Pennway bent grass, with Penncross bent on the tees and greens, which are protected by a watering system that sprays mist to lower the air temperature on hot days. The man responsible for the superb condition is superintendent Bill Knox, who for five years was first assistant at Augusta National, where he learned his trade.

The course is private, for members and their guests only. "We're member-sensitive," Waddy Stokes said. "We're not trying to please everyone. We have seven or eight groups playing on a fairly busy weekday. On weekends we'll probably have fifty to sixty players per day." And then he added something that I'd been waiting a long, long time to hear: "We try to space it so there is never more than one group on a hole."

Lake Toxaway
Country Club

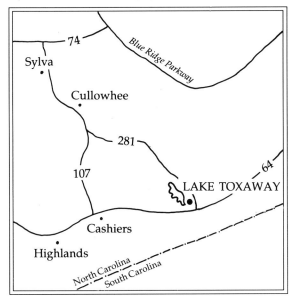

Box 70
Lake Toxaway, North Carolina 28747
704-966-4260

Private

Joe Lee, designer

Course Ratings

Blue 69.1
White 68.0
Red 68.1

PHOTOGRAPH BY CHIP HENDERSON COURTESY OF THE LAKE TOXAWAY COMPANY

Located on North Carolina's largest private lake, the Greystone Inn is the most elegant small inn in the entire Southeast. Not only is it beautiful to look at and wonderful to stay in for a weekend or a week, it enjoys a rich history of entertaining such name brands as Henry Ford, Thomas Edison, and John D. Rockefeller. In recognition of exceptional quality, the Greystone is North Carolina's only country inn to be a recipient of the AAA Auto Club's Four Diamond Award.

The one drawback to this charming place is that there are only twenty rooms in the mansion, with another twelve in the lakefront Hillmont Inn. Each room comes with a spacious deck that overlooks the lake, a fireplace, a wet bar, and a large luxury bath with a Jacuzzi.

One of the amenities is that each day at sunset, you can join the Greystone's owner, Tim Loveless, an outgoing and agreeable chap, on a party-boat cruise aboard his twenty-eight-foot Mountain Lily II. Loveless knows every bit of history and folklore about this spectacular country, the exotic lake, and the first-class golf course that begins about two hundred yards down the hill. Another custom is afternoon tea, which is served on the inn's sun porch, resplendent with white wicker furniture.

I've stayed at the Greystone twice now, but with all the other things to do, I've only played the course at the Lake Toxaway Country Club once. It's a short course, but it's very demanding. The 6,003 yards from the blues or the 5,516 from the whites will lull you to sleep when you start off. But then all of a sudden, when you think you're playing low-80s golf, you're in the 90s. The course rolls through the mountains that surround the lake, and I had a lot of side-hill lies and a lot of long downhillers. One hole, the 13th, comes in at 659 from the back tees, but since it's downhill, you can get there with two woods and a long iron.

Normally, I play a high shot and have difficulty keeping the ball low. I think everyone does.

HOLE NUMBER	1	2	3	4	5	6	7	8	9	OUT	10	11	12	13	14	15	16	17	18	IN	TOT	HCP	NET
BLUE TEES	445	165	275	311	141	342	332	438	238	2687	315	378	429	659	230	375	132	438	360	3316	6003		
WHITE TEES	425	160	261	285	135	327	313	408	190	2504	293	331	401	535	205	354	124	420	349	3012	5516		
HANDICAP	3	16	17	14	15	12	13	8	10		11	5	2	1	6	9	18	4	7				
PAR	5	3	4	4	3	4	4	5	3	35	4	4	4	5	3	4	3	5	4	36	71		
RED TEES	402	145	235	266	121	286	275	381	185	2296	278	304	241	408	150	258	114	401	276	2430	4726		
HANDICAP	3	12	17	10	16	11	7	6	9		8	2	14	1	13	15	18	5	4				
PAR	5	3	4	4	3	4	4	5	3	35	4	4	4	5	3	4	3	5	4	36	71		

Anyhow, at Toxaway I was able to hit away and let the ball go as high as it wanted. There's nothing quite like watching a really good drive hang in the air for five or six seconds and then see it bounce and roll another forty yards. After my round, I joined Tim Loveless and his guests on the sun porch, where the golfers compared scorecards, settled bets, and exchanged drinks.

There is a note on the bottom of the Greystone mailer that reads, "State law does not allow us to sell alcoholic beverages, but we provide set-ups and your private storage locker for beverages you choose to bring." So you have to do two things: make your reservations very early and bring your own bottle.

KENMURE GOLF CLUB

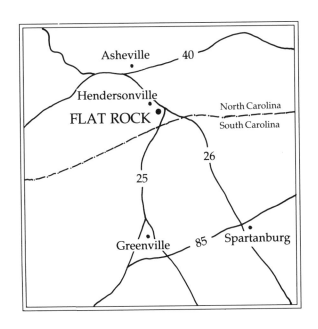

100 Clubhouse Drive
Flat Rock, North Carolina 28731
704-693-8481

Semi-Private

Joe Lee, architect

Course Ratings

Back 71.5
Middle 69.8
Front 70.3

COURTESY OF KENMURE GOLF CLUB

One afternoon, Bill Robinson, a former Florida attorney and developer, was asked by two Hendersonville bankers to take a look at a run-down golf and residential area south of Flat Rock, part of the area called "the little Charleston of the mountains" in the early part of the nineteenth century. Robinson walked up to the porch of the white mansion on the hill overlooking the golf course and gazed through the window into a room that once sparkled with chandeliers and Oriental rugs and prosperous Charlestonians who had come to the mountains to escape the heat and the humidity. The inside was barren, but the chipped wallpaper, the broken windows, and the dust weren't all that Robinson saw. "It was a beautiful old home even though it was run-down," he said. "And the land around it was ideal for a golf resort."

Today at Kenmure, located just a few miles down the road from the historic Flat Rock Playhouse and the home where Carl Sandburg spent his later years, the scene has shifted dramatically. Bill Robinson can now look out of his office on the third floor of the mansion on the hill and see one of the most beautiful and best-kept courses in the Carolinas. He can see a swimming pool, tennis courts, and the 18th hole of a truly great golf course. The most striking aspect of the view may be the fairways, with their contrasting bands of light and dark green cutting diagonally across the playing areas. The look is achieved by the costly and time-consuming practice of having individual mowers crisscross the fairways instead of using tractors pulling five or six wide blades.

It was in 1985 that Robinson joined forces with Lee King and Jim Floyd, two locals, and Ben Wright, the golf writer and broadcaster. Together they decided to make Kenmure into an internationally famous course, and together they set about doing it. In 1987, the reshaped and rebuilt course was the scene of the North

HOLE NUMBER	1	2	3	4	5	6	7	8	9	OUT	10	11	12	13	14	15	16	17	18	IN	TOT	HCP	NET
BACK	384	535	425	392	168	321	359	507	171	3262	523	163	342	532	196	354	349	389	399	3247	6509		
MIDDLE	366	513	406	374	149	310	343	491	137	3089	490	136	331	513	174	341	326	365	382	3058	6147		
PAR	4	5	4	4	3	4	4	5	3	36	5	3	4	5	3	4	4	4	4	36	72		
HANDICAP	9	3	1	7	15	17	13	5	11		4	16	18	2	10	12	14	8	6				
FRONT	295	475	346	311	138	295	257	441	108	2666	399	125	316	439	126	267	296	317	307	2592	5258		
PAR	4	5	4	4	3	4	4	5	3	36	5	3	4	5	3	4	4	4	4	36	72		
HANDICAP	9	3	5	7	15	17	13	1	11		4	16	18	2	10	12	14	8	6				

Carolina Open. The open came back in 1988, and today Kenmure is recognized as one of the premier courses in the Carolinas.

While most courses have bluegrass on the fairways and bent grass on the greens, Kenmure has bent-grass fairways. The result is a lush playing surface that gives you a perfect lie every shot. Even if you shoot 100, rolling your ball to a better lie is a waste of time.

Beyond the feel of the course, there is a wonderful look about Kenmure that you won't find anywhere else. For the first nine holes, you see the mountains. For the back nine, you play through them. But perhaps the best drawing card at Kenmure, along with the beautiful course, the French chef, and the freshly cut roses on the tables in the dining room, is the simple fact that it's open all year. The secret is that Kenmure's elevation is lower than that of other mountain courses, and its winters aren't as severe.

As Bill Robinson said, "There are days when we have to close, but there are many very nice days in the middle of the winter when it's absolutely beautiful here. Just bring a sweater. Ben Wright and I will guarantee you a good tee time."

The Grove Park Inn
And Country Club

290 Macon Avenue
Asheville, North Carolina 28804
704-252-2711

Semi-Private

Donald Ross, designer

Course Ratings

Blue 69.4
White 67.5
Red 68.5

COURTESY OF THE GROVE PARK INN AND COUNTRY CLUB

OK. What did the following name brands have in common: Will Rogers, Bobby Jones, Mikhail Baryshnikov, William Jennings Bryan, F. Scott Fitzgerald, Enrico Caruso, Herbert Hoover, Calvin Coolidge, and Harry Houdini? Answer. They all stayed at the Grove Park Inn. They all didn't play golf on the famous Donald Ross course that starts right outside the doorway, but they all stayed and ate at the inn, and according to the old gravure prints in the lobby, they kept coming back. And when they did, they walked the incredible boulder-lined hallways and warmed their feet in front of one of the fireplaces that can hold twelve-foot logs, supported by andirons weighing five hundred pounds each.

The owner and founder of the Grove Park Inn was none other than Mr. E. W. Grove himself, the man who gave the world Grove's Chill Tonic and Grove's Bromo Quinine, two patented formulas he developed while he was a small-town druggist in Paris, Tennessee. As a matter of fact, Grove, not a modest man, wrote the inn's origi-

nal ad: "The finest resort hotel in the world has been built at Sunset Mountain, Asheville, North Carolina."

Grove's claim may still hold true. Since its 1913 opening, the Grove Park Inn has been a favorite hideaway for honeymooners and celebrities alike. It has also received Mobil's coveted Four Star Award and the AAA Auto Club's Four Diamond Award. A $65 million restoration has just been completed on the old place, which has amenities that include carriage rides, swimming pools inside and out, tennis facilities, four restaurants, a nightclub, and nine boutiques. In 1984, the inn's size was doubled to 510 rooms, with 42 meeting rooms. Along with the course, it is now open all year.

Down the hill from the inn is one of the most famous Donald Ross courses ever built. Opened in 1909 as the Asheville Country Club, it is the region's oldest golf course and one of Ross's first. Ross built his courses only on the finest land and did everything he could to preserve the

HOLE NUMBER	1	2	3	4	5	6	7	8	9	OUT	10	11	12	13	14	15	16	17	18	IN	TOT	HCP	NET
BLUE	392	196	487	453	428	341	214	496	204	3211	501	343	187	332	356	114	421	435	401	3090	6301		
WHITE	371	177	461	425	412	311	191	478	173	2999	482	326	161	324	324	106	405	414	384	2926	5925		
MEN'S HDCP.	9	17	3	5	1	7	13	11	15		6	8	16	14	2	18	10	4	12				
MEN'S PAR	4	3	5	5	4	4	3	5	3	36	5	4	3	4	4	3	4	5	4	36	72		
RED	339	147	389	353	393	241	124	352	140	2478	416	258	137	289	303	97	348	377	284	2509	4987		
LADIES' HDCP.	11	13	1	7	3	9	15	5	17		4	8	16	14	6	18	10	2	12				
LADIES' PAR	4	3	5	5	5	4	3	5	3	37	5	4	3	4	4	3	4	5	4	36	73		

natural terrain. At the Grove Park Inn and Country Club, you can see his early work, and you will come to love the sweep and the nuances that characterize it. Any Donald Ross course is a joy to play, but this one is special because it was built long before bulldozers and long before anyone had the idea that a golf course should be a good real-estate investment and an attraction for homebuilders. For a great weekend during any time of the year and a chance to play on one of the best courses in the country, you can't go wrong here.

ELK RIVER CLUB

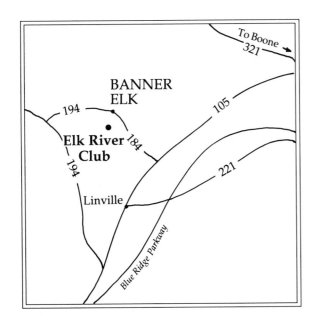

P.O. Box 1555
Banner Elk, North Carolina 28604
704-898-9777

Private

Jack Nicklaus, designer

Course Ratings

Championship Blue 72.9
Member's White 70.3
Senior's Yellow 67.8
Women's Red 70.2

PHOTOGRAPH BY BRIAN MORGAN COURTESY OF ELK RIVER CLUB

1 4 2

Elk River Club, just down the road from the Linville Golf Club, is the newest addition in the Blue Ridge, brought to you by none other than Mr. Jack Nicklaus himself. Elk River is the first and probably the only course in the country to have its own airport. As a matter of fact, you have to go under the landing strip to get to the course. Once there, you will find spread out in front of you one of the most beautiful vistas in the country.

The course is not an easy one, and unless someone holds a gun to your head, avoid the back tees. Nicklaus designed Elk River for his kind of game. But as Bobby Jones once remarked, "Mr. Nicklaus plays a game of which I am unfamiliar." So unless you're out there 240 to 260, forget the tips. Many of the landing areas simply can't be reached by anyone but a big, big hitter or someone playing an illegal ball.

On the other hand, and the important hand, the course was built for the members, not the pros, and from the white tees it's a great test of

your game and a great layout. I've played Elk River just once, and only by hitting thirteen greens did I score an 87. My troubles came on the greens. But the course was great, and it was fair. A bad shot will invariably cost you another shot, but good shots are never punished.

Looking down the fairways, you'll see that the mowing stripes are matched up the way the material is in an expensive cut of clothes. Now that's what I call an eye for detail. And if your game goes sour, as it will on occasion, and you've ever thought about taking Walter Hagen's advice to slow down and smell the flowers, Elk River, with breathtaking mountains in the background and slopes covered with laurel and rhododendron, is the place to do it. Much like Grandfather Golf and Country Club, Linville Ridge, and Linville Golf Club, Elk River is blessed with scenery that you will find absolutely nowhere else in the U.S. of A.

Pete Dye says the eye can't see a 2½-inch fall over ten feet. But the breaks are there at Elk

HOLE NUMBER	1	2	3	4	5	6	7	8	9	OUT	10	11	12	13	14	15	16	17	18	IN	TOT	HCP	NET
BLUE	376	392	175	326	467	180	512	360	553	3341	474	212	555	394	429	497	369	161	414	3505	6846		
WHITE	359	374	161	301	394	164	492	345	502	3092	439	195	491	343	388	480	349	140	377	3202	6294		
YELLOW	321	325	121	287	378	151	427	319	463	2792	402	172	453	309	343	464	307	129	341	2920	5712		
MEN'S HCP.	11	5	15	13	9	17	3	7	1		2	16	6	14	4	10	12	18	8				
PAR	4	4	3	4	4	3	5	4	5	36	4	3	5	4	4	5	4	3	4	36	72		
RED	292	305	96	237	318	140	398	278	442	2506	382	119	433	285	321	379	281	116	320	2636	5142		
WOMEN'S HCP.	11	5	15	13	9	17	3	7	1		2	16	6	14	4	10	12	18	8				

PHOTOGRAPH BY BRIAN MORGAN
COURTESY OF ELK RIVER CLUB

River, because Jack Nicklaus built the greens to discourage twenty-footers from going straight in. So the only way to know the breaks is to play the greens several times. That is the advantage club members have over guests and even over visiting pros. Anyhow, with the built-in microscopic falls, plus the fact that the slope of the mountain pushes the ball off line, putting at Elk River is something you have to learn. So if you play the course, don't expect too many long putts to drop, and if you have a few three-putts, don't let them bother you. It happens to all of us. Over and over and over again.

P.O.Box 1348
Linville, North Carolina 28646
704-898-4531

Private

Ellis Maples, designer

Course Ratings

Back tees 54.4
Front tees 54.0

PHOTOGRAPH BY HUGH MORTON COURTESY OF GRANDFATHER GOLF AND COUNTRY CLUB

Great mountain courses are rarities in the United States, and Grandfather Golf and Country Club is just that, a rarity. It lies at the base of Grandfather Mountain, right across the road from the Linville Ridge course and about four miles from Linville Golf Club. And when you add in Elk River, a few more miles away, you're talking about a lot of championship golf in a very small area in Avery County. Maybe Palm Beach has a heavier concentration of championship courses, but Palm Beach doesn't have the mountains, and Palm Beach doesn't have the views or the rivers.

Grandfather Mountain is the highest peak in the Blue Ridge Mountains, and in the spring and the fall there is no prettier place on earth. There are two courses at this private club, both designed and built by Ellis Maples. The championship course is consistently rated one of the finest mountain courses in the Carolinas, or for that matter, in the world.

Grandfather Golf and Country Club is, of course, much more than just a couple of great courses. It is a wildlife sanctuary complete with bears, raccoons, deer, and every other furry creature of the night. Activities include indoor and outdoor tennis, trout fishing, and sailing. But why a dedicated golfer would lay down his sticks and play tennis or go boating or trout fishing when he could play golf on this magnificent layout is beyond my comprehension.

I've played here only once, and I'm here to report that the layout is absolutely superb. While I had a good score from tee to green, I had at least eight three-putt greens. Which brings me to a travel tip I'd like to point out. If you play here, be careful on the greens. And be prepared for them. As everybody knows, a green near a mountain breaks away from the mountain. But knowing that and putting it into practice are two very different things. The only way you can conquer this phenomenon is to get out on the practice green and really work on it. No matter how hard I tried, when I had a five-footer that looked

HOLE NUMBER	1	2	3	4	5	6	7	8	9	OUT	10	11	12	13	14	15	16	17	18	IN	TOT	NET
BACK TEES	156	270	157	148	287	139	92	118	98	1465	153	276	286	172	140	145	253	181	155	1761	3226	
HANDICAP	5	3	11	7	1	9	17	13	15		8	6	2	10	18	16	4	12	14			
PAR	3	4	3	3	4	3	3	3	3	29	3	4	4	3	3	3	4	3	3	30	59	
FRONT TEES	92	187	133	99	210	104	92	101	98	1116	131	260	202	106	115	108	214	125	127	1388	2504	
LADIES HDCP.	13	3	5	9	1	11	15	7	17		8	4	6	14	18	12	2	16	10			

PHOTOGRAPH BY HUGH MORTON
COURTESY OF GRANDFATHER GOLF AND COUNTRY CLUB

straight, it was still almost impossible to allow two or three inches for the break. So when a putt looks straight, do what Bernhard Langer does, only do it quicker. Back off, look around, and see exactly where the mountain is, then allow at least two inches. It will look weird and it will feel weird and you will probably adjust your direction on the downswing and aim right for the hole, and then you will miss it. But don't say you weren't warned.

Linville Golf Club

Pisgah
National
Forest

P.O. Box 98
Linville, North Carolina 28646
704-733-4363

Private

Donald Ross, designer

Course Ratings

Long 72.0
Regular 69.6
Ladies 69.3

9TH GREEN

PHOTOGRAPH BY HUGH MORTON COURTESY OF LINVILLE GOLF CLUB

On August 30, 1794, André Michaux, French botanist and explorer, ascended Grandfather Mountain and recorded in his journal, "Climbed to the summit of the highest mountain of all North America with my guide, and sang the Marseillaise Hymn, and cried, 'Long live America and the French Republic! Long live Liberty!'"

However, it was left to a very famous American philosopher, William James, to record more specifically the peculiar inspiration that the town of Linville and Grandfather Mountain gave to visitors. In 1891, he noted, "At last, I have struck it rich here in North Carolina and am in the most peculiar and one of the most poetic places I have ever been. Strange to say, it is on the premises of a land speculation and would-be boom. . . . Not a loafer, not a fly, not a blot upon the scene. The serpent has not yet made his appearance in this Eden, around which stand the hills covered with primeval forest of the most beautiful description. . . .

"Apparently the company has just planted a couple hundred thousand dollars in pure esthetics, a most high-toned proceeding in 'this degenerate age.' Later, doubtless a railroad, stores, and general sordidness will creep in. Meanwhile, let us enjoy things!"

Well, William James would be pleased if he could see just how little has changed at the old Linville Golf Club. The first golf course here was built in the late 1890s, which brings it in right around the time St. Andrews in Yonkers was laid out. Nothing else happened until 1920, when the company in charge engaged the services of Pinehurst's Donald Ross to build the course that is still with us today. Ross took a team of surveyors with him into the woods and rhododendron thickets and completed his work in only two days. He left and later sent back the plans from his office. When they were laid out, they fit the topography perfectly. Donald Ross's work has not been drastically changed, and to-

HOLE NUMBER	1	2	3	4	5	6	7	8	9	OUT	10	11	12	13	14	15	16	17	18	IN	TOT	HCP	NET
LONG COURSE	405	395	449	565	400	195	343	532	169	3453	331	427	222	560	157	506	325	384	415	3327	6780		
REG. COURSE	350	360	414	521	342	175	316	514	150	3149	305	422	175	538	135	495	315	357	395	3137	6286		
MEN'S HDCP.	9	7	1	5	11	15	13	3	17		14	2	16	4	18	8	12	10	6				
PAR	4	4	4	5	4	3	4	5	3	36	4	4	3	5	3	5	4	4	4	36	72		
LADIES COURSE	335	335	337	395	250	135	211	437	130	2565	225	354	135	403	100	445	222	290	347	2521	5086		
LADIES HDCP.	7	9	1	5	13	15	11	3	17		14	4	16	6	18	2	12	10	8				

18TH GREEN

PHOTOGRAPH BY HUGH MORTON
COURTESY OF LINVILLE GOLF CLUB

day Linville Golf Club is probably the most prestigious private club in North Carolina.

While the facilities at Linville Golf Club are
reserved for members, guests of the Eseeola
Lodge may also play. Since the Eseeola Lodge
remains busy without doing any advertising, the
message is clear that interested parties should
sign up as early as possible, like tomorrow
morning.

LINVILLE RIDGE

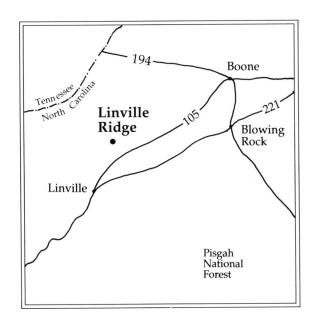

P.O. Box 704
Linville, North Carolina 28646
704-898-5151

Private

George Cobb, designer

Course Ratings

Men's Blue 71.8
Men's White 69.5
Men's Gold 67.4
Women's Red 68.5
Women's Gold 72.3

7TH HOLE

PHOTOGRAPH BY HUGH MORTON COURTESY OF LINVILLE RIDGE

It's hard to believe, but little Avery County in western North Carolina, with only three stoplights, has the highest concentration of championship golf courses of any place in the Carolinas. Not even Myrtle Beach, Pinehurst, or Hilton Head can match it in the ratings. So much for firsts.

Most mountain courses are really valley courses running through the mountains. The result is that while golfers are surrounded by mountains, they play on fairly flat holes with little or no elevation between tee and green. Linville Ridge is different. Instead of looking up at the mountains they are playing through, golfers can look down from them. With its five-thousand-foot elevation, Linville Ridge is the highest course east of the Rockies, and it is quite simply breathtaking.

George Cobb, the architect who took three years to build the course, put his thumb right on it when he said, "The scenery here is absolutely fantastic, but we can't take all the credit for that.

God's the one who created that and you have to give Him credit. . . . But we were working really closely with Him."

Linville Ridge's clubhouse, the highest in the eastern United States and the largest in the Carolinas, is surrounded by camellias and roses, and the mountain slopes around it are covered with laurel and rhododendron. In the spring, it's a festival; in the fall, a circus. And year-round in the evenings, you can watch the clouds shifting below and the colors changing in the sky above, while in the distance the dying sun plays its reds and yellows and golds over the face of old Grandfather Mountain.

Golf Digest has rated Linville Ridge the fourth best course in North Carolina, while *Golf Reporter* has rated it second. The holes are spectacular, but the one that impressed me the most was the 7th, a downhill 183-yarder where club selection can run from a 5-iron to a full 3-wood, depending on the wind. And while you're trying to decide which club to hit and where to hit your

HOLE NUMBER	1	2	3	4	5	6	7	8	9	OUT	10	11	12	13	14	15	16	17	18	IN	TOT	HCP	NET
BLUE	398	413	400	504	167	363	199	497	410	3351	581	389	205	393	395	210	302	393	517	3385	6736		
WHITE	378	390	380	475	142	340	183	483	378	3149	525	347	164	339	354	194	286	368	484	3061	6210		
GOLD	369	339	357	437	115	320	172	459	348	2916	475	328	121	316	322	176	276	325	458	2797	5713		
MEN'S HDCP.	7	13	1	9	17	11	15	3	5		10	16	18	12	4	6	14	2	8				
PAR	4	4	4	5	3	4	3	5	4	36	5	4	3	4	4	3	4	4	5	36	72		
RED	311	313	297	374	111	274	153	431	317	2581	433	299	101	283	276	126	259	232	424	2433	5014		
LADIES HDCP.	7	9	3	11	17	13	15	1	5		8	14	18	10	2	16	4	12	6				

10TH HOLE

PHOTOGRAPH BY HUGH MORTON
COURTESY OF LINVILLE RIDGE

shot, you can look out over the ridges seventy-five miles into the great state of Tennessee.

The brilliant white sand that surrounds the 7th and all the other holes at Linville Ridge is from nearby Spruce Pine. It is the same sand used by Augusta National for the Masters. In other words, Linville Ridge has spared no expense, and the result is a masterpiece.

Even if it's raining or snowing, my advice is to come and play anyway. On clear days, you'll want to finish off your round by sitting in the lounge with your favorite drink and watching the sunset, for this is a truly spectacular course in a truly spectacular setting.

Tanglewood
CHAMPIONSHIP COURSE

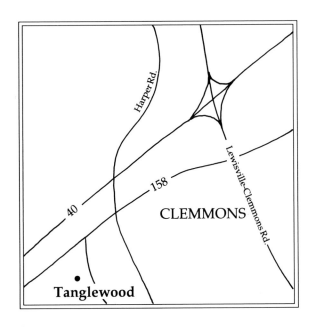

Highway 158, P.O. Box 1040
Clemmons, North Carolina 27012
919-766-0591

Public

Robert Trent Jones, designer

Course Ratings

Championship 74.5
Middle Back 72.8
Middle Front 70.1
Ladies 70.9

COURTESY OF TANGLEWOOD PARK

I've never seen anything quite like the Tanglewood Championship Course Robert Trent Jones built in Clemmons, North Carolina. First of all, the view from the clubhouse out over the incredible sweep of land with the beautiful fountain in the center is a sight I will not soon forget. The Championship Course not only hosted the 1974 PGA Championship, won by Lee Trevino, and the 1986 USGA Public Links Championship, it is today the home of the celebrated Vantage Golf Championship. But there's a catch. This is a public golf course. A public course where a high or low handicapper can walk onto the 1st tee and tee up for seventeen dollars and play one of the best courses in the country.

Bobby Vaughan, the vice-president of golf operations at Tanglewood, said, "I don't think there is a golf course anywhere in the world that a local citizen can play of this caliber at our price."

Golf magazine named the 5th hole here as one of the most challenging in the United States, and *Golf Digest* ranked the course among the top twenty-five publics, and a strong candidate to enter the top hundred public or private.

Robert Trent Jones, who also built the lush and very sporty eighteen-hole Reynolds Course and the superb driving range and putting green at Tanglewood, said it simply: "In my opinion, the [Championship Course] is one of the greatest golf courses we've ever done. I think it should be ranked in the top hundred in the country, maybe even in the top twenty. . . . I love this course, and I think we've made it so that it can host any sort of major championship but at the same time it can be enjoyed by the weekend golfer."

And a quote from Walt Zembriski, the man who won the Vantage in 1988: "I've played public courses since I was eleven years old. [This] is the finest public course I've ever played."

Recently, the R. J. Reynolds Tobacco Company spent almost a million dollars on improvements, especially on the greens, which they con-

HOLE NUMBER	1	2	3	4	5	6	7	8	9	OUT	10	11	12	13	14	15	16	17	18	IN	TOT	HCP	NET
CHAMPIONSHIP	375	190	444	400	608	387	243	440	439	3526	364	490	235	418	424	367	183	580	435	3496	7022		
MIDDLE BACK	364	178	421	382	575	372	208	420	419	3339	344	467	210	395	383	359	183	540	418	3199	6538		
MIDDLE FRONT	347	161	389	362	556	290	190	400	399	3094	327	393	182	330	336	330	135	500	387	2920	6014		
HANDICAP	11	17	3	9	1	13	15	5	7		14	4	16	10	6	12	18	2	8				
PAR	4	3	4	4	5	4	3	4	4	35	4	4	3	4	4	4	3	5	4	35	70		
FRONT	330	130	327	342	500	260	162	292	379	2722	281	337	130	291	266	291	112	400	289	2397	5119		
LADIES PAR	4	3	4	4	5	4	3	5	5	37	4	5	3	4	4	4	3	5	5	37	74		

COURTESY OF TANGLEWOOD PARK

verted from Bermuda to bent grass. Zembriski liked the alterations. "Those greens are perfect now," he said. "I liked them before simply because I like fast greens, but they've got a lot more grass on them now. The new rolls and swales will make the course play even tougher."

I arrived here one day at five o'clock, and carrying about half of my sticks, I played the front nine with a sweet-potato broker. The guy had the fastest backswing I've ever seen, but somehow at the last split second, he made some seismic correction that got the club face in square, and he was 250 yards off every tee. Unfortunately, when he picked up an iron, any iron, he turned to stone, and the eights and nines came rolling in. But he never complained, and he swore to me that he was enjoying every hole.

While I only played nine holes that day, I had a great time. Tanglewood is a very friendly place, and it's easy picking up a playing partner hanging around the driving range or the putting green. I also had a very good chicken-salad sandwich and a cold beer in the lounge when I finished. All in all, the Tanglewood Championship Course is a wonderful layout, and if the signs said private instead of public, and the green fees were a hundred dollars instead of seventeen dollars, it would still be one of the best golf bargains in the Tar Heel State.

FOREST OAKS COUNTRY CLUB

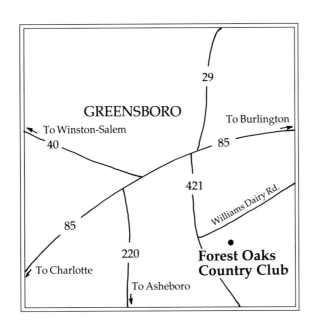

4600 Forest Oaks Drive
Greensboro, North Carolina 27406
919-674-0127

Private

Ellis Maples, designer

Course Ratings

Blue 73.9
White 70.9
Red 69.6
Gold 68.8

8TH HOLE

PHOTOGRAPH BY DEAN CROUCH   COURTESY OF FOREST OAKS COUNTRY CLUB

If you think the only place where Ben Hogan, Byron Nelson, Sam Snead, Arnold Palmer, and Seve Ballesteros have all prevailed is the Masters, you're only half right—those same players have also won the Greater Greensboro Open (GGO).

To begin at the beginning, the Starmount Forest Country Club hosted the Carolina Open in 1932, and the king of the pros, Walter Hagen, was expected to win easily. But it didn't work out quite that way. A Mr. Henry Picard, who was later to show up in South Carolina as pro of the Charleston Country Club, beat him soundly.

In any event, it was that tournament, plus the fact that Tony Manero—the pro at the Sedgefield Country Club in Greensboro—captured the 1936 U.S. Open, that proved the germ of the GGO, catapulting the city into one of the golf capitals of the country.

When the original GGO was organized in 1938 by the local Jaycees to promote the city, it was played on two courses, Starmount and Sedge-

field. Here is a quote from Jaycee member Archie Joyner about organizing the event: "It was suggested we call the Jaycee members and see how many of them would underwrite $25. We got on the phone and raised $750 or $800. I don't think any of us had $25 but we pledged it anyway. We had a prospectus that showed 150 golfers would be in town for four days, and they would spend $5 a day while here. They would also use caddies, and at $1 a round, that's another $600 in the local economy. Things were tough back then."

During the tournament, the participants played two days at Starmount, then the Jaycees moved everything across town to Sedgefield on Sunday night. "[We] had a beautiful scoreboard, and . . . a flatbed truck," Joyner said. "We took off for Sedgefield, going out Merritt Drive, and there was the underpass at Pomona. It wouldn't go under. It was screwed down, rather than nailed, so we went back to that hardware store at Pomona, bought six or seven screwdrivers—all

HOLE NUMBER	1	2	3	4	5	6	7	8	9	OUT	10	11	12	13	14	15	16	17	18	IN	TOT	HCP	NET
BLUE	393	383	186	503	438	554	408	188	426	3479	407	511	409	190	415	386	372	215	574	3479	6958		
WHITE	367	337	165	450	403	522	377	155	395	3171	369	479	368	152	377	349	343	179	539	3155	6326		
GOLD	328	331	139	445	391	480	347	140	363	2964	359	470	349	150	365	339	330	165	511	3038	6002		
HANDICAP	9	13	17	15	5	1	7	11	3		10	18	2	16	6	8	14	12	4				
PAR	4	4	3	5	4	5	4	3	4	36	4	5	4	3	4	4	4	3	5	36	72		
RED	322	319	139	418	302	415	212	132	312	2562	344	405	270	106	348	285	294	154	484	2690	5252		
LADIES' HCP.	7	13	17	3	11	1	15	9	5		8	10	4	18	6	12	14	16	2				

12TH HOLE

COURTESY OF FOREST OAKS COUNTRY CLUB

they had—and took out the three hundred or so screws so we could get under the underpass. Then we put it up again, an hour or more each time. We had a few beers. It must have been 8 A.M. before we finished." Such was the beginning of what has turned out to be one of the premier tournaments on the PGA tour.

In 1966, Forest Oaks Country Club became a qualifying site for the GGO, and in 1977 the tournament moved here, where it has remained ever since. The GGO, which has seen most of its winners go on to win the Masters, is played every year a week or so before or after the Masters. It is a great event, and the list of famous players who have played in the tournament goes on and on.

I played Forest Oaks once in the spring, when the whole countryside was in bloom, and the wide-open fairways, the beautiful greens, and the sweeping landscape reminded me a lot of Augusta. The course is a wonderful layout for its eight hundred members, and from the back tees the pros have to hit a steady string of great shots to get around in 72. Forest Oaks is truly one of the best courses in the Carolinas, and the GGO, thanks to the tireless and unselfish help of the Jaycees, is certainly one of our finest tournaments.

PINEHURST
HOTEL & COUNTRY CLUB

COURSE NUMBER 2

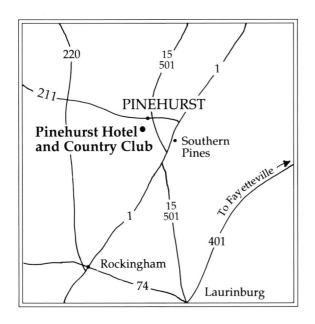

P.O. Box 4000
Pinehurst, North Carolina 28374
1-800-672-4644

Semi-Private

Donald Ross, architect

Course Ratings

Back 73.5
Middle 71.0
Ladies 73.5

17TH HOLE

PHOTOGRAPH BY JIM MORIARTY COURTESY OF PINEHURST HOTEL AND COUNTRY CLUB

About ten years back, I played Pinehurst Number 2 the way Snead and Hogan and Byron Nelson played it. I played it from the back tees. I had a caddie and I walked every great foot of it. As a matter of fact, I had Snead's old caddie, Junior, who told me anything and everything I wanted to know about golf and Pinehurst and Mr. Snead himself.

From the tips, the course is 7,020 yards, with a USGA rating of 73.5. The tee elevations are slightly higher than those for the middle tees, and the landing areas are dramatically different. Second and third shots can get very difficult. I had been warned how hard the course is, but I wouldn't listen, and I went out in something around 45 and came in pretty close to 50, for a not-so-sparkling 95, a score I never posted or told too many people about.

With the simpleminded reasoning common to most golfers, I reasoned that I hadn't properly appreciated the old course with a 95, so I tried the middles. And I was right. I had a decent 85,

and it was amazing what a difference it made. The first thing I noted was that except for the 16th, there is no water. The second was that if you get in trouble, you can, with an exceptional shot, get out of it. The third thing was that if you stay in or near the middle and you can putt, you can score. But you must putt well.

While Number 2 doesn't have the spectacular views and landscapes of, say, Grandfather Golf and Country Club, or the pelicans, alligators, and Spanish moss of Hilton Head, it has something altogether different. What that is I can't quite put my finger on, but I think it's the way Donald Ross used the landscape without changing it. As you walk along, you get the feeling that you're seeing the land the way it was a hundred years ago, and the way it will be forever. Ross used only mules and drags to shape the land when he built the course over fifty years ago, and it is amazing how it has withstood the test of time.

The last time I was at Pinehurst, Don Padgett,

HOLE NUMBER	1	2	3	4	5	6	7	8	9	OUT	10	11	12	13	14	15	16	17	18	IN	TOT	HCP	NET
BACK	396	441	335	547	445	212	401	487	166	3430	578	433	415	374	436	201	531	190	432	3590	7020		
MIDDLE	378	414	317	477	427	195	372	455	147	3182	459	410	351	345	412	188	470	162	390	3187	6369		
HANDICAP	11	3	13	5	1	15	9	7	17		2	8	10	14	4	16	12	18	6				
MEN'S PAR	4	4	4	5	4	3	4	5	3	36	5	4	4	4	3	5	5	3	4	36	72		
LADIES'	361	394	302	449	417	178	320	429	127	2977	443	363	335	325	395	161	415	149	371	2957	5934		
HANDICAP	9	7	13	3	1	15	11	5	17		2	10	12	14	6	16	4	18	8				
LADIES' PAR	4	4	4	5	5	3	4	5	3	37	5	4	4	4	5	3	5	3	4	37	74		

16TH HOLE

PHOTOGRAPH BY JIM MORIARTY
COURTESY OF PINEHURST HOTEL AND COUNTRY CLUB

the golf director, walked me around the club-house, which looks out over five of the seven courses, and showed me exactly how Ross built a green. From a hundred yards away, Padgett can look at a green and tell you if it's a Donald Ross, and if not, why not.

If you come to Pinehurst—and as a golfer you must come to Pinehurst—you've got to try Number 2 from the back tees just to see what happens. And after you tear up your 95 or 100, then play it again from the middle tees, the way Donald Ross meant for you to play it. It's a course you will never, ever forget. Number 2 is often described as one of the most difficult courses in the world from within fifty yards of the green. So sharpen up your bump-and-run shots and smooth out that putting stroke.

PINEHURST
HOTEL & COUNTRY CLUB

COURSE NUMBER 4

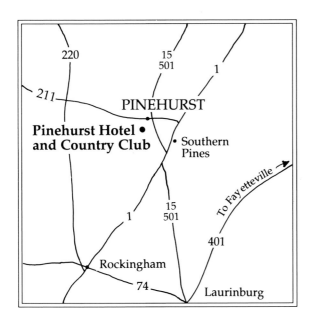

P.O. Box 4000
Pinehurst, North Carolina 28374
1-800-672-4644

Semi-Private

Robert Trent Jones and Donald Ross, architects

Course Ratings

Back 73.6
Middle 71.5
Ladies 73.0

12TH HOLE

PHOTOGRAPH BY JIM MORIARTY COURTESY OF PINEHURST HOTEL AND COUNTRY CLUB

From the middle tees, Pinehurst Number 4 is 6,371 yards, with a USGA rating of 71.5, which makes it exactly half a stroke harder than Number 2. I don't happen to believe that, but this is not the time or the place to be arguing with the USGA.

The reason for the difficulty is that while Number 4 is another Donald Ross course, it was originally only 6,000 yards, and it was later modified and toughened up. In 1973, Robert Trent Jones significantly lengthened the course so it could be used in the World Cup Open. And then in 1983, Rees Jones softened it up a bit again and made it, in his words, "a fairer test for the high handicappers, yet still a challenging course for the long hitters."

With the old Donald Ross greens, which were basically flat with hog-backed characteristics, the ball would simply roll off the putting surface if not struck exactly right. The greens have since been enlarged from forty-five hundred to six thousand square feet, and they undulate with as many as three putting tiers.

From an architectural standpoint, the modifications have taken out a few of the severe penalties for the average golfer, yet the course still requires accurate club selection, precise handling of the short game, and good putting.

Number 4 is a solid course with good elevations from the tees and wonderful greens. There are only two holes where water comes into play. But once again, this is a course where you must place your shots.

Of the seven courses at Pinehurst, five can be seen from what is probably the most beautiful clubhouse in the South. It looks a great deal like the clubhouse out in the hills of Shinnecock. And if you sit on the veranda and watch the action on the 1st tees and 18th greens that surround you, you will be watching from where Teddy Roosevelt, Dwight Eisenhower, Bobby Jones, and Francis Ouimet once sat.

HOLE NUMBER	1	2	3	4	5	6	7	8	9	OUT	10	11	12	13	14	15	16	17	18	IN	TOT	HCP	NET
BACK	431	181	486	441	371	192	382	519	399	3402	428	210	520	163	390	366	418	547	446	3488	6890		
MIDDLE	395	153	460	400	341	150	363	453	390	3105	399	181	482	142	374	351	405	506	426	3266	6371		
HANDICAP	5	17	9	1	13	15	11	7	3		6	10	4	18	14	16	12	2	8				
MEN'S PAR	4	3	5	4	4	3	4	5	4	36	4	3	5	3	4	4	4	5	4	36	72		
LADIES'	350	145	410	312	316	135	343	443	374	2828	375	130	425	98	357	337	358	446	372	2898	5726		
HANDICAP	7	17	1	13	11	15	9	5	3		10	16	4	18	12	14	8	2	6				
LADIES' PAR	4	3	5	4	4	3	4	5	4	36	5	3	5	3	4	4	4	5	4	37	73		

PINEHURST RESORT CLUB

A great tradition at Pinehurst, and one that is vanishing much too quickly from the American scene, is the presence of caddies. More than forty caddies work at the club—in the old days there were over five hundred—and all you have to do is ask for one. Don Padgett, the golf director, makes it a point to try and get players visiting for the first time to take a caddie and walk the course.

Every time I play here I use a caddie, and to this day every one of them has known more about the old Royal and Ancient than I'll ever know. Junior, Snead's old caddie, seemed to know every shot in the rainbow, including one with a 9-iron that he called his "balloon shot." He also had a grip, a swing, and a finish that I would kill for.

PINEHURST
HOTEL & COUNTRY CLUB

COURSE NUMBER 6

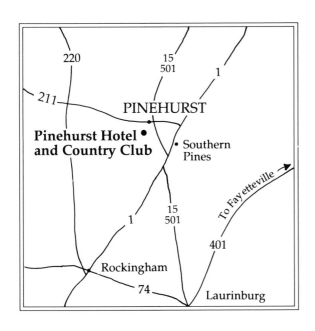

220
15
501
1
211
PINEHURST
Pinehurst Hotel
and Country Club
Southern
Pines
To Fayetteville
1
15
501
401
Rockingham
74
Laurinburg

P.O. Box 4000
Pinehurst, North Carolina 28374
1-800-672-4644

Semi-Private

George and Tom Fazio, architects

Course Ratings

Back 74.5
Middle 71.0
Ladies 71.5

9TH HOLE

PHOTOGRAPH BY JIM MORIARTY COURTESY OF PINEHURST HOTEL AND COUNTRY CLUB

Designed and built by George and Tom Fazio in 1980, Pinehurst Number 6 is three miles from the main clubhouse. Number 6 differs from the other Pinehurst courses in its tight fairways, which wind through the oaks and pines and cedars. A typical hole like the par-5 10th calls for a tee shot down a narrow fairway. The next shot narrows between two lakes, which must be carried. If you negotiate both shots, your approach shot is uphill to a long, narrow green heavily bunkered on the left. It is not an easy hole. When you play Number 6, be sure and use a caddie. You will need all the help you can get in selecting clubs and judging distances.

A few of the caddies have been here since the early days of Pinehurst. Leon Dawson, one of the oldest and one of the best, recalled, "I was nine years old the first time I ever went out. The golf bags were small then—they didn't have the big trunks they use today, but were mainly of canvas with about seven or eight wooden clubs, nine at the most. All of the greens were sand.

Anyhow, this man I caddied for looked at me. I was so small the bag was dragging the ground, so he tied it up for me, with a big knot so it didn't drag. He'd also pull out and carry two or three clubs in his hand so the bag wouldn't be so heavy. We kids got fifty cents for an eighteen-hole loop back then. Later, during the big Depression, Pinehurst started making their own money, you know, tokens. You could spend these at the Pinehurst company stores in the village. You couldn't buy cigarettes or chewing tobacco, just staple items."

I grew up caddying in Columbia, and some of the best times I've ever had at Pinehurst have been trading stories with caddies like Leon, Junior, and a few of the others. Here's another quote from Leon: "A really good golfer never gets overconfident—he stays humble—and he works hard. Now, Walter Hagen would have two or three doubles before he began to play. But after he started you'd never know it—he was just that smooth. Those were the good old

HOLE NUMBER	1	2	3	4	5	6	7	8	9	OUT	10	11	12	13	14	15	16	17	18	IN	TOT	HCP	NET
BACK	430	523	198	413	406	520	212	370	437	3509	552	409	427	210	393	526	230	417	425	3589	7098		
MIDDLE	388	461	169	347	370	471	187	334	401	3128	480	380	369	188	347	479	189	363	391	3186	6314		
HANDICAP	7	3	17	9	11	1	15	13	5		2	12	8	18	14	4	16	10	6				
MEN'S PAR	4	5	3	4	4	5	3	4	4	36	5	4	4	3	4	5	3	4	4	36	72		
LADIES'	328	419	135	264	332	400	133	286	365	2662	415	341	347	134	322	435	103	316	325	2738	5400		
HANDICAP	7	1	17	11	9	3	15	13	5		2	10	8	18	6	4	16	14	12				
LADIES' PAR	4	5	3	4	4	5	3	4	4	36	5	4	4	3	4	5	3	4	4	36	72		

days with all those old-timers. I loved it. It was great to see the way they played golf. Things were easy, and in a way, I think you could say there was a lot of romance to the whole thing."

When you come to Pinehurst, you'll discover your own kind of romance, but be sure and ask for a caddie. And if you're lucky, maybe you'll get Leon or one of his buddies. You won't regret it.

1OTH HOLE

PHOTOGRAPH BY JIM MORIARTY
COURTESY OF PINEHURST HOTEL AND COUNTRY CLUB

PINEHURST
HOTEL & COUNTRY CLUB

COURSE NUMBER 7

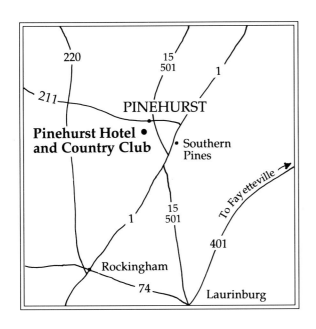

P.O. Box 4000
Pinehurst, North Carolina 28374
1-800-672-4644

Semi-Private

Rees Jones, architect

Course Ratings

Gold 75.0
Blue 73.5
White 70.4
Silver 69.0

13TH HOLE

COURTESY OF PINEHURST HOTEL AND COUNTRY CLUB

Located on a 393-acre tract of land just south of the PGA World Golf Hall of Fame and about a half-mile from the main clubhouse is the newest addition to the family of interconnected golf courses in the Sandhills at Pinehurst. Once again, the influence of Donald Ross's traditional design is evident, as the three-year-old Pinehurst Number 7 winds its way over rolling terrain, native marshes, and streams. The only features missing are Ross's greens.

The course, which measures 7,114 from the back tees, was designed by Rees Jones, who said, "In designing Number 7, the key emphasis was in working with the site's diverse natural-terrain features. The championship length may seem long but many of the holes are downhill from the tee, allowing it to play much shorter."

In general, Number 7 is much hillier than the other courses at Pinehurst, and it also presents a different appearance on almost every hole. It flows easily from a Scottish design, with pot bunkers, grassy hollows, swales, and mounds, to that of a mountain course, with sudden, dramatic changes in elevation.

Of particular note is the 10th hole, which features no fewer than ten pot bunkers. The spectacular 13th, a gorgeous hole, requires a carry over a natural berm nearly twenty feet high to an elevated, well-bunkered green.

Perhaps the most outstanding aspect of Number 7, and what makes it so unforgettable, is the incredible variety of the terrain. Groves of poplar and dogwood trees, along with the never-ending tall pines, frame many of the holes, and in the spring this may be the most beautiful course at Pinehurst.

The only time I played Number 7, I played from the middle tees. But on the 13th, a par-3 measuring 203 yards, I pulled out my 2-iron and decided to go from the back. I hit a career shot stiff to the flag, and I went whistling down the middle of the fairway carrying only a putter and

HOLE NUMBER	1	2	3	4	5	6	7	8	9	OUT	10	11	12	13	14	15	16	17	18	IN	TOT	HCP	NET
GOLD	514	452	405	423	201	447	388	530	204	3564	393	407	546	203	387	427	196	395	596	3550	7114		
BLUE	493	419	380	404	181	422	378	515	181	3373	370	385	529	186	354	406	177	369	570	3346	6719		
WHITE	460	399	363	388/358	150	384/360	355/322	500	157	3156/3069	347/319	339	477/447	161	324/302	379	151/123	357	525	3060/2952	6216/6021		
HANDICAP	7	1	11	9	17	3	13	5	15		14	8	4	16	12	6	18	10	2				
PAR	5	4	4	4	3	4	4	5	3	36	4	4	5	3	4	4	3	4	5	36	72		
SILVER	416	320	288/271	328	98	289	256	409	117	2521/2504	260	262	410	88	287	292	90	257	457	2403	4924/4907		
HANDICAP	3	7	11	5	17	9	13	1	15		14	10	4	16	6	8	18	12	2				

thinking birdie. And from twenty-five feet, I went for it. Unfortunately, it didn't go for me. Two putts later, I had a bogie.

It's been a couple of years since I hit that 2-iron, and I can still see the configuration of the clouds that framed the hole, and the great way the ball faded into the center of the green and bounced toward the flag. The three putts have vanished long ago, but my 2-iron shot will always remind me that my all-time favorite hole at Pinehurst has to be the 13th on Number 7.

Landfall

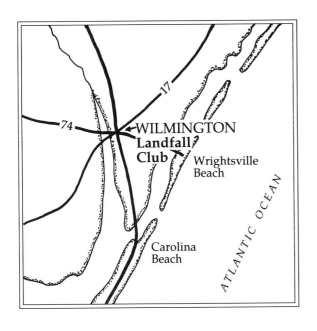

1801 Eastwood Road
Wilmington, North Carolina 28405
1-800-634-7857 in NC
1-800-227-8208 outside NC

Private

Pete Dye, designer

Course Ratings

Gold 73.9
Blue 72.3
White 69.5
Silver 66.4

COURTESY OF LANDFALL CLUB, INC.

In the Wilmington area, the nights are colder and the oaks and sycamores are taller than along the South Carolina coast. The possum and the coon have given way to the groundhog, the skunk, and the bear, and if you're not careful, you'll get served home fries for breakfast instead of grits. As for golf courses, bent-grass greens flourish in the cooler weather, and while you can't play as many days as you can at, say, Dataw Island or Seabrook Island, you can certainly play most days. All of which brings me in the side door to the Landfall Club, a facility that, frankly, I find hard to believe. I've never seen anything quite like it.

To begin at the source is to begin with Pembroke Jones, the man who owned the Standard Rice Company. While Jones made his fortune in New York City, his heart never left his native Wilmington. In 1902, he acquired fifteen hundred acres of land on Wrightsville Sound and started construction on two homes. And what homes they were. The first was Airlie,

which even today, almost ninety years later, is known for the breathtaking, expansive gardens of azaleas Mrs. Jones planted and nurtured. The other home was Pembroke Park, a hunting lodge and estate dedicated to the pursuit of enjoyment.

From atop their walled perch beside the main gates, two life-sized marble lions greeted visitors to Pembroke Park. At the lodge, another set of lions roared their welcome. Statues lined the narrow paths, and a domed and columned gazebo overlooked a well-stocked freshwater lake. Quail, duck, wild turkey, and deer abounded in the forest, while bear haunted the swamp. One tale has it that Jones and his guests dined in the limbs of a giant oak—table, silver, champagne, and all—by the light of the shimmering moon to the musical accompaniment of old-time spirituals. Today, only the gazebo still stands, but what has been added would surely please the exotic taste of Pembroke Jones. The area now called Landfall encompasses the same

HOLE NUMBER	1	2	3	4	5	6	7	8	9	OUT	10	11	12	13	14	15	16	17	18	IN	TOT	HCP	NET
GOLD	388	403	563	206	466	335	184	459	502	3506	373	129	463	521	402	530	431	211	431	3491	6997		
BLUE	376	388	535	200	436	321	168	443	487	3354	350	122	425	507	385	512	401	194	419	3315	6669		
WHITE	354	332	484	166	390	288	143	385	465	3007	316	115	394	496	363	490	379	166	384	3103	6110		
SILVER	320	292	460	153	332	235	111	325	451	2679	284	104	341	485	338	415	322	141	366	2796	5475		
HANDICAP	11	9	5	15	1	13	17	3	7		14	18	2	10	12	8	4	16	6				
PAR	4	4	5	3	4	4	3	4	5	36	4	3	4	5	4	5	4	3	4	36	72		
RED	260	269	416	143	317	225	96	310	400	2436	274	66	275	400	282	405	266	124	316	2408	4844		

fifteen hundred acres, with three miles fronting the Intracoastal Waterway.

An outstanding Pete Dye Course has been built at Landfall, and a Jack Nicklaus Course will be opening in the near future. No expense has been spared and no detail has been overlooked in making Landfall absolutely luxurious. Penncross bent grass carpets the greens, hybrid Bermuda sweeps across the fairways, and centipede tests the unfortunate golfer in the rough.

The practice tee is over 300 yards long and 150 yards wide, with large tees at each end. It is equipped with four target greens, practice bunkers, and a chipping green. With the Pete Dye Course and the Jack Nicklaus Course and the miles of rolling hills overlooking the waterway, Landfall will not only be a golfing haven unrivaled on the coasts of both Carolinas, it will fulfill the promise of the grand life that Mr. and Mrs. Jones started here in 1902.

BALD · HEAD · ISLAND

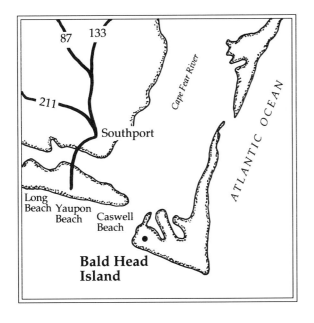

87   133

211

Cape Fear River

Southport

ATLANTIC OCEAN

Long
Beach Yaupon
Beach   Caswell
Beach

**Bald Head
Island**

P.O. Drawer 10999
Bald Head Island, North Carolina 28461
1-800-722-6450 in NC
1-800-443-6305 outside NC

Semi-Private

George Cobb-course consultant

Course Ratings

Men's Blue 73.0
Men's White 70.5
Ladies Red 68.5
Ladies Yellow 67.5

PHOTOGRAPH BY RON CHAPPLE COURTESY OF BALD HEAD ISLAND

Kent Mitchell, who with his brother Mark directs the operations at Bald Head Island, summed up the family philosophy in the following way: "On so many of America's barrier islands one hears the sad refrain, 'I wonder what this island was like when it was still innocent.' When Mark and I first saw Bald Head, we recognized that here was a barrier island which had somehow managed to be touched by civilization, yet not ruined by it. From the beginning, we were determined to preserve the island's profound sense of innocence. . . . Frankly, those who view beach resorts like Hilton Head, Myrtle Beach, and Miami Beach as paradises wouldn't care for the lifestyle at Bald Head Island."

George Cobb, the architect who designed and built the course at Bald Head Island, seems to have felt the same way as the brothers Mitchell, for he has carved a remarkable course out of the sand dunes, live oaks, palm clusters, and huge bay trees. From almost every vantage point, only a few houses are visible. Freshwater lagoons curve lazily through fourteen of the fairways, and when the wind comes up, scores can skyrocket.

The greens are incredible, averaging eleven thousand square feet, and while they are fast and true, they also undulate. I've played the course five times now, and the one tip I can pass on is to avoid hooking at all costs. There are fourteen holes where water comes into play on the left side, and it's just waiting for you the way it was waiting for me.

One great thing about Bald Head Island is that no cars are allowed. Once you are off the ferry that leaves from Southport, the only way you can get around is by golf cart. Each villa comes equipped with one. So after you play golf on the really superb layout, you can drive your cart back to your room, clean up, and then drive through a tunnel of trees in the maritime forest to a fabulous restaurant that specializes in local seafood and continental dishes. The island is also famous for its turtle-conservation program,

HOLE NUMBER	1	2	3	4	5	6	7	8	9	OUT	10	11	12	13	14	15	16	17	18	IN	TOT	NET
BLUE TEES	400	200	390	505	450	420	510	180	435	3490	430	500	430	220	430	420	200	480	440	3550	7040	
WHITE TEES	360	180	360	485	420	390	470	155	400	3220	390	470	400	166	390	370	170	450	410	3216	6436	
HANDICAP	16	18	6	4	8	12	10	14	2		11	15	5	9	1	17	3	13	7			
PAR	4	3	4	5	4	4	5	3	4	36	4	5	4	3	4	4	3	5	4	36	72	
RED TEES	290	140	280	405	340	320	370	115	315	2575	310	390	290	98	315	300	110	380	325	2518	5093	

and no visit is complete without a nighttime turtle walk with the resident zoologist.

For a truly relaxing spot where you can literally get away from everything and still play all the golf you want on a superb course, you would have to go a long way to beat Bald Head Island. And while you're here, be sure and buy one of the famous blue jackets they sell in the pro shop.

As if all this isn't enough of a good thing, the Mitchells, living up to their promise, are developing only two thousand of the nearly thirteen thousand acres on Bald Head Island. They have donated the remaining eleven thousand acres to the state of North Carolina as a preservation site. Now if only a few more developers would follow their example.

PLANTATION

Shallotte

17

904

**Brick Landing
Plantation**

179

Ocean Isle
Beach

Calabash

Sunset
Beach

ATLANTIC OCEAN

Route 2, Box 210
Ocean Isle Beach, North Carolina 28469
1-800-222-9938 in NC
1-800-438-3006 outside NC

Public

H. Michael Brazeal, designer

Course Ratings

Blue 71.5
White 69.4
Gold 67.8
Red 67.8

PHOTOGRAPH BY CURTIS MYERS COURTESY OF BRICK LANDING PLANTATION

Historically, Brick Landing Plantation was the site where bricks from England were unloaded by colonists building their homes and communities in seventeenth-century America. Remnants of the old ferry system can still be seen, and an oak-shaded trail once used by mule-drawn wagons laden with bricks still exists. Today, the beautiful site is the home of a championship golf course that looks out over the Intracoastal Waterway, the tidewater marshlands, and an endless sweep of magnolias, live oaks, and sweet gums.

The designer of the course, H. Michael Brazeal, explained the plan: "My goal was to integrate the many unique features with the sound principles of golf course design and construction, so that we could create a world-class facility. I think we have succeeded."

Four holes at Brick Landing are on the waterway, four more are on the marsh with views of Saucepan Creek, and the rest weave through natural forests dotted with lakes, ponds, and lagoons.

When *Golfweek Magazine* listed its fifty most distinctive courses in the Southeast, Brick Landing was right there with North Carolina's finest—Linville Ridge and Pinehurst Number 7. The course is only 6,482 yards from the back tees, while it's 6,154 from the front. But if you think 6,154 is easy, Brick Landing will prove you wrong. With water on seventeen holes, the only way to break 90 is with the head and not the big swing. So when you come here, plan your shots carefully. Another good tip is to leave your driver in the car and use a 3-wood off the tee. You lose twenty yards or so, but it's a small price to pay to avoid the penalties you can pick up with a stray drive.

A couple of years back, Brick Landing introduced one of the most exciting tournaments on the amateur scene. Any amateur can enter. All you need is a pair of shoes, a set of sticks, and a handicap of three or under. And all you have to do

HOLE NUMBER	1	2	3	4	5	6	7	8	9	OUT	10	11	12	13	14	15	16	17	18	IN	TOT	HCP	NET
TOURNAMENT	369	119	345	510	424	365	563	173	456	3324	357	359	153	513	351	501	438	121	365	3158	6482		
MEMBER	356	112	332	495	403	338	536	148	431	3151	337	339	145	498	326	481	421	116	346	3003	6154		
SENIOR	329	107	319	480	380	301	503	137	408	2964	321	312	134	459	310	459	409	110	314	2828	5792		
HANDICAP	9	17	11	1	7	13	3	15	5		12	2	16	10	14	4	6	18	8				
PAR	4	3	4	5	4	4	5	3	4	36	4	4	3	5	4	5	4	3	4	36	72		
LADIES	255	101	280	428	282	287	449	122	299	2503	257	265	127	379	250	400	292	87	275	2332	4835		

PHOTOGRAPH BY CURTIS MYERS
COURTESY OF BRICK LANDING PLANTATION

is call for details and show up around the Fourth of July. The 1989 winner, Gary Robinson, won with an even-par score of 288. As an indication of just how hard the course is, the runner-up, Larry Penley, the golf coach at Clemson, holds the course record with a 68. I played here once, and my foursome out of Wildwood in Columbia and Palmetto in Aiken might have beaten Larry Penley's record with our best-ball net. All we had to do was hole a few seventy-footers.

Oyster Bay
Golf Links

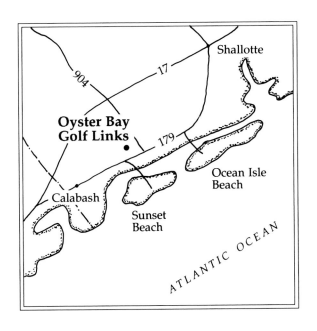

P.O. Box 65
North Myrtle Beach, South Carolina 29597
1-800-552-2660

Semi-Private

Dan Maples, designer

Course Ratings

Tournament Gold 74.1
Blue 72.9
White 70.2
Red 69.1

17TH HOLE

COURTESY OF OYSTER BAY GOLF LINKS

From a low-flying plane, Oyster Bay Golf Links looks more like a water-skiing playground than a golf course. I've never seen so much water. I don't mean creeks and little ponds, I mean huge, gaping lagoons and full-blown lakes and a stretch of the Intracoastal Waterway that must be as wide as the Mississippi.

The course opened in 1983, and only two years later, after it had had time to mature, *Golf Digest* wisely named it the best new resort course in the country. To me, Oyster Bay is one of the most beautiful and most diversified courses this side of Torquebrada in southern Spain.

An example of its distinctiveness is its trademark oyster shells, which are built into almost everything. The par-3 17th is played from an oyster-shell-walled tee onto an island green built on a mountain of shells. The 13th, which measures only 330 from the back tees and 320 from the middle, is played along a lake that skirts the entire right side, across a cavernous bunker, to a wickedly undulating green that rests on an oyster-shell wall. The wall rises white and stark out of the lake and is a graphic example of this unique and innovative concept.

Oyster Bay, located at Sunset Beach, is a classic creation of architect Dan Maples and developer Larry Young. Their fresh approach to design and their use of oyster shells is carried over in the beautiful clubhouse, which contains a complete pro shop, a restaurant, a third-floor lounge, and an atrium.

I've played the course only once, and after a not-so-hot round, I discovered that my favorite spot was the third-floor lounge, where I enjoyed a cold beer. After reexamining my card and realizing that my five sixes and one seven should have all been fives, and that my true score should have been close to an 82 instead of a 94, I penciled in my revised score and got a total stranger to attest to it. Then, as I watched the sun setting over a sweet gum tree that sagged under the weight of what looked like a hundred egrets, and as I convinced myself that I'd really

HOLE NUMBER	1	2	3	4	5	6	7	8	9	FRONT	10	11	12	13	14	15	16	17	18	BACK	TOT	HCP	NET
GOLD	390	450	470	190	550	165	390	160	560	3325	440	450	370	330	535	210	470	165	400	3370	6695		
BLUE	380	420	420	180	530	155	380	150	550	3165	430	430	360	320	525	205	450	165	385	3270	6435		
WHITE	340	385	365	160	510	125	370	135	490	2880	395	415	315	300	510	135	375	100	365	2910	5790		
MEN'S HDCP.	7	1	3	11	9	17	13	15	5		4	6	18	14	16	8	2	10	12				
PAR	4	4	4	3	5	3	4	3	5	35	4	4	4	4	5	3	4	3	4	35	70		
RED	265	320	285	135	380	95	275	100	450	2305	250	360	260	230	410	85	360	75	295	2325	4630		
LADIES HDCP.	11	7	5	15	1	17	9	13	3		2	4	18	10	12	14	6	16	8				

shot an 82 out there among the shells and over the water, I decided that Oyster Bay is the course and the place I want to come back to again and again and again.

Marsh Harbour
golf links

Shallotte

904   17

Marsh Harbour Golf Links

179

Calabash

Ocean Isle Beach

Sunset Beach

ATLANTIC OCEAN

P.O. Box 65
North Myrtle Beach, South Carolina 29585
803-249-3449

Semi-Private

Dan Maples, designer

Course Ratings

Blue 73.3
White 70.0
Red 69.0

17TH TEE

COURTESY OF MARSH HARBOUR GOLF LINKS

Like Oyster Bay, Marsh Harbour Golf Links, which sits right on the border between North and South Carolina, is a creation of architect Dan Maples and developer Larry Young. Opened in 1980, it was ranked eighth in the Carolinas by the Carolina PGA professionals that very same year. Since then, it has become one of the most popular courses on the coast. While Marsh Harbour measures only 6,000 from the middle tees, it could very well be the hardest 6,000-yard course in the country. There are no easy shots. I've played Marsh Harbour only once, and after snaking in a few long putts, I came in with an 84 that I will long treasure.

I especially liked the 7th, 8th, and 9th, which are billed as Amen Corner. On the 10th, a good drive with a fade will go from North Carolina across a historic boundary marker into South Carolina before landing safely on the fairway back in North Carolina. Incidentally, Marsh Harbour is about a drive and a 3-wood south of Calabash, which has long been famous for its great "Calabash-style" seafood.

Marsh Harbour has some wild holes, but the wildest is the 17th. Billed as "the challenge of a lifetime" and "the most beautiful and exciting hole" in the Grand Strand area, the 17th lives up to its press. It's a par-5 510-yarder featuring three distinct target areas, each getting smaller and more difficult. Off the tee to the right are large bunkers and the marsh. On the left are tall pines and oaks. Once you've driven safely, you'll find yourself drying your hands and thinking about using an old ball. On the second shot, you have to cross another treacherous stretch of marsh and water to a peninsula of fairway. The landing area is fairly generous, but on the right side is a trap that will catch anything short. In any event, once you are on the peninsula, you're faced with still another peninsula and the hardest shot. It's about a 140- or 150-yard 6- or 7-iron to a green precariously perched on the side of the marsh. If

HOLE NUMBER	1	2	3	4	5	6	7	8	9	FRONT	10	11	12	13	14	15	16	17	18	BACK	TOT	NET
BLUE TEES	370	375	520	240	370	210	390	210	540	3225	410	190	500	390	220	420	435	570	330	3465	6690	
WHITE TEES	325	320	475	190	330	175	360	170	510	2855	365	155	475	365	180	385	400	510	310	3145	6000	
HANDICAP	14	16	18	6	12	8	10	4	2		9	11	17	15	5	7	3	1	13			
PAR	4	4	5	3	4	3	4	3	5	35	4	3	5	4	3	4	4	5	4	36	71	
RED TEES	310	270	415	120	270	150	300	145	460	2440	325	70	350	300	130	350	300	330	200	2355	4795	

you hit this shot, you will have hit three great shots in a row—which I did—and you'll probably think you deserve a birdie—which I also did. But the bad news is that you'll probably suffer the same fate I did. I had a twenty-footer for a bird, but the green has an undulation in it that requires a degree of wisdom I didn't have that day. Anyhow, three putts for a bogie on the 17th wasn't all that bad.

All in all, Marsh Harbour is a great course to play, because it will stretch the limits of your long game *and* your short game.

The Pearl
Golf Links

Route 8, Sunset Lakes Boulevard
Calabash, North Carolina 28459
919-579-8131

Public

Dan Maples, designer

Course Ratings

East Course:
Black 73.1
Blue 72.1
White 70.8
Gold 68.4
Pink 73.9

West Course:
Black 73.2
Blue 72.5
White 71.0
Gold 68.0
Pink 73.4

PHOTOGRAPH BY MICHAEL SLEAR COURTESY OF BRANDON ADVERTISING

Much like Linville, in the North Carolina highlands to the west, Calabash, just up the road from the Grand Strand, is rapidly becoming a great golf center. *Becoming* may be the wrong word here, because with the opening of the Pearl Golf Links, a thirty-six-hole layout soon to become seventy-two, the Calabash area can already contend with every major golf center in the country.

While most course owners are interested in selling off a string of lots and eventually going semiprivate or private, the owners of the Pearl have decided to stay public, a very wise decision because it has allowed them to build a clubhouse with the public, and only the public, in mind.

And what a clubhouse. Despite the Pepto Bismol pink that was the unfortunate color choice, the clubhouse is still elegant and tastefully appointed. After a round, you can have a meal or sit in a very comfortable lounge and watch ball games on a panoramic six-foot TV screen. And if you've lost the rent money on skins or a Nassau bet, you might be able to get it back playing pool on the full-sized table under a chandelier that looks like it came off the set of *Gone With the Wind*. All in all, the clubhouse combines the casual atmosphere of a public course with the elegance of the most lavish private clubs on the circuit.

Keith Clearwater, no slouch on the PGA tour, is the touring pro playing out of the Pearl, and two or three days a week you'll find him on the driving range or the putting green doing whatever pros do to hold their fine edge. And speaking of driving ranges, the Pearl has the best one I've seen at a public course in the entire state. As for the putting green, it's centrally located, and the beautifully kept bent grass is exactly like the grass on the big, undulating greens out on the courses.

The staff at the Pearl goes beyond being friendly and courteous to do everything possible to make sure you have a pleasant round. They will help you with tee times, and if you show up

East Course

HOLE NUMBER	1	2	3	4	5	6	7	8	9	OUT	10	11	12	13	14	15	16	17	18	IN	TOT	HCP	NET
BLACK	533	200	349	416	208	394	412	353	510	3375	398	324	185	521	177	421	358	418	572	3369	6749		
BLUE	523	186	339	405	195	381	399	340	501	3269	385	311	171	506	166	415	352	406	562	3274	6543		
WHITE	506	171	327	381	185	357	384	322	481	3114	361	294	152	485	155	402	341	396	550	3136	6250		
GOLD	476	145	315	346	165	326	351	292	463	2879	329	271	120	442	142	361	316	369	527	2877	5756		
HANDICAP	10	3	16	8	7	2	4	15	13		12	14	17	9	18	6	11	5	1				
PAR	5	3	4	4	3	4	4	4	5	36	4	4	3	5	3	4	4	4	5	36	72		
PINK	457	130	285	289	145	284	311	264	438	2603	303	214	93	430	129	316	273	336	428	2522	5125		

alone, as I did, they will hook you up with another loner looking for a game. They will also help you with your game and your equipment. In my case, my car battery went dead in the parking lot, and within minutes one of the staff showed up in a pickup truck waggling a pair of jumper cables.

The two courses now in play at the Pearl were designed and built by Dan Maples. The West Course measures 6,738 from the middle tees, while the East Course comes in at 6,543. Both are superb, laid out on land that has a definite Scottish-links look, with clumps of lovegrass, pot bunkers, and sand traps everywhere. As a matter of fact, if you stand at the clubhouse, you can look out across both courses and see most of the holes.

West Course

HOLE NUMBER	1	2	3	4	5	6	7	8	9	OUT	10	11	12	13	14	15	16	17	18	IN	TOT	HCP	NET
BLACK	391	205	556	167	431	358	579	215	458	3362	394	358	401	147	614	443	604	151	534	3646	7008		
BLUE	364	190	546	157	411	349	568	195	425	3207	367	349	390	138	605	436	584	139	523	3531	6738		
WHITE	359	180	531	148	386	336	551	183	391	3065	349	338	356	135	571	407	556	134	508	3354	6419		
GOLD	336	145	485	125	360	318	512	169	358	2808	320	313	315	122	507	370	475	124	467	3013	5821		
HANDICAP	10	5	13	16	2	14	12	7	3		11	15	8	18	6	4	1	17	9				
PAR	4	3	5	3	4	4	5	3	4	35	4	4	4	3	5	4	5	3	5	37	72		
PINK	255	115	456	111	358	280	442	128	307	2452	310	275	279	109	466	338	436	95	428	2736	5188		